FROM
DACHAU
TO D-DAY

FROM DACHAU TO D-DAY

THE REFUGEE WHO FOUGHT FOR BRITAIN

HELEN FRY

The History Press

First published 2009

The History Press
The Mill, Brimscombe Port
Stroud, Gloucestershire, GL5 2QG
www.thehistorypress.co.uk

British Library Cataloguing in Publication Data.
A catalogue record for this book is available from the British Library.

ISBN 978 0 7509 5111 1

Typesetting and origination by The History Press
Printed in Great Britain

DEDICATION

Dedicated to David and Anthony Field, their wives,
children and grandchildren

*'I was part of the 8th King's Royal Irish Hussars,
the famous Desert Rats, and nothing could take away the feeling of
exhilaration at being part of such a regiment.'*
Willy Field

CONTENTS

ACKNOWLEDGEMENTS

I would like to express my heartfelt thanks to Willy Field for sharing his life story with me and enabling me to write this book. It has been a privilege for me as a historian to record his oral testimony and work on the life of an extraordinary man. This book could not have been written without the unquestionable support of his wife Judy and their sons David and Anthony. My sincere thanks to each of them for their enthusiasm and practical support. I would also like to thank Willy's twin sister, Dorothea, for help with material and memories for the book.

Willy and I would like to thank a special group of veterans, some of whom Willy has known for over sixty years, for their continued support of my research and their interest in this book. They are Harry Rossney, Geoffrey Perry, John Langford, Bill Howard, Peter Eden, Frank Berg, Leo Dorffman, Ralph Fraser, Hans Jackson, Fred Gillard and Rudy Karrell. We would also like to express our deep appreciation to Gabriele Wasser, the schoolteacher in Bonn, for providing detailed information about her educational school projects with Willy in Germany. We would also like to thank Willy's close friend and fellow veteran Gerry Moore with whom he was in Australia and then the British forces. Gerry has kindly recalled many events and memories of their time together for the purpose of this book.

A special mention is due to Sophie Bradshaw, an exceptional Commissioning Editor, whose insight and vision have enabled stories to be published which may otherwise not have seen the light of day. That is true also for the immense dedicated support I have received over the last year from Peter Teale. He has supported my ideas and brought some of them to fruition. It is fun and stressfree working with him. Thanks to Simon Hamlet and the editorial team at The History Press for producing such a quality publication and with whom it has been a real pleasure to work. I also wish to acknowledge the idiosyncratic Paul Savident whose support of my writing projects in so many diverse ways is much appreciated.

Thanks to Mick Catmull of BBC South-West who produced a remarkable documentary about the *King's Most Loyal Enemy Aliens* for the regional *Inside Out* programme. Willy featured as the central veteran who was interviewed in that documentary. It was screened on BBC South-West on 16 October 2006 and also on national BBC on Remembrance Sunday, November 2006.

Huge thanks to the dedicated, experienced team at True North Productions who made a documentary, 'Churchill's German Army', which featured Willy and was broadcast on the National Geographic Channel on 26 April 2009. The team flew Willy back to Holland where he lost his whole tank crew in action sixty-five years earlier.

Sincere thanks are due also to Suzanne Bardgett, Director of the Holocaust Office at the Imperial War Museum, for her friendship and continued support to me in this field of research. I would like to acknowledge Colonel John Starling and Norman Brown of the Royal Pioneer Corps Association for their interest and support of my books. Thanks to Dirk Riedel of the archives of Dachau Concentration Camp Memorial Site for information; also to German journalist Matthias Martin-Becker, based in Berlin, who has taken an active interest in these veterans' stories, including a couple of interviews for radio and newspapers about Willy. He has portrayed the story with sensitivity and accuracy. I have been fortunate to have the support and encouragement of staff at The Association of Jewish Refugees, including Howard Spier, Hazel Beiny and Esther Rinkoff. Thanks to Marian Strnavsky for supporting my writing. Ever grateful thanks to Alexia Dobinson for typing up the interviews and war diaries for this book.

Mary Curry of Barnstaple is to be accredited with starting off a whole series of books which I have written in recent times, including some contracted in the foreseeable future. Back in 2001 she posed one question to me which started off a chain of books – what had I done about researching the Jewish refugees in North Devon during the Second World War? It turned out that there had been over 3,000 of them – a large percentage of whom were the intellectuals of Germany and Austria who were forced to flee Nazi oppression, one of them being Willy Field. Little did we know then that her question would lead to the recording of a virtually undocumented period of refugee-Jewish history. Mary has read and commented on every draft of the chapters for this book, and for that I am immensely grateful and could not do without her critical eye and sharp mind.

I have an exceptional network of friends who continue to support my work. To them, I owe a huge debt of gratitude: to my loyal friend James Hamilton who has built up a remarkable creative and dynamic partnership with me on writing historical novels under the pseudonym of J.H. Schryer; also to Louisa Albani, Elkan Levy, Colin Hamilton, Evelyn Friedlander, Edith Palmer and Richard Bernstein.

This book could not have been written without the support of my family: my husband Martin, our sons Jonathan, David and Edward, and my mother Sandra. Thank you. During the writing of this book and during the years of friendship with Willy, my sons who are avid Arsenal F.C. supporters have benefited from football mementos and Arsenal memorabilia which Willy has so generously given.

INTRODUCTION

Seated beside me in a smart relaxed living room in a leafy suburb of north-west London is a white-haired gentleman whose fit and youthful countenance belies his age. He is just a year from his ninetieth birthday. Over the previous five years he and his wife have become very special friends to me. This elderly British citizen has an extraordinary tale to tell me. He was not born in England but Germany. His was a happy childhood in Bonn in the early years of the twentieth century, until his dreams were shattered by Hitler's ascent to power in 1933. As a Jew, he and his family lived the next few years in constant fear for their lives. Living in the shadow of the swastika and all that it stood for was a daily reality. It is now an aeon away, and yet for him, it seems like yesterday.

At the dining-room table, he waits for us to start the next interview. All his papers, documentation and photos are spread out in front of us. He is one of 'my men' as I call them – one of the 10,000 German and Austrian refugees from Nazism who fought for Britain in the Second World War. I am struck by his humility and modest claims not to have done very much in the war. 'I am no war hero', he tells me. But when I discuss his wartime contribution and experiences, I discover that behind his kind and gentle demeanour hides decades of suffering and loss inflicted by the Nazis. It also conceals six years of selfless sacrifice, two of which were spent fighting on the front line in France, Belgium, Holland and Germany after D-Day. He is a man with 'nine lives', having survived extraordinary circumstances against the odds. Willy was incarcerated in Dachau concentration camp for four months in 1938–9, came to England, was interned a year later and survived the torpedoing of the troopship *Dunera* which carried him to Australia in 1940. Later, he was the sole survivor of his crew when his tank was hit by German fire on the road between Eindhoven and Nijmegen in the Netherlands in September 1944. Working through the war diaries and official regimental history of the 8th King's Royal Irish Hussars with whom he served as a tank driver, I became aware of just how dangerous it was for Willy and his comrades fighting on the front line. The 8th Hussars played a leading role, with other tank and infantry regiments, in spearheading the advance through Normandy into the Netherlands and Germany. It was a surprise for me to learn that when Willy and his regiment finally entered Germany, the country was not in complete disarray. German defeat seemed assured, but the last die-hard Nazis defended their country to the bitter end. Thus Willy and his comrades experienced some of the toughest front-line fighting in Germany. After the war he discovered that all his family had perished in the Holocaust, except sister Thea who was in England.

One could understand perfectly well if Willy harboured resentment, bitterness or desire for vengeance towards the perpetrators. He does not – and in that sense he is an extraordinary human being, one who has reflected on his experiences and chosen a path of forgiveness. In spite of personal suffering at the hands of the Nazis, he bears no grudges. He is philosophical about the need to forgive, but never to forget the past. After the war, he became a British citizen and has lived a life of total loyalty to this country. He is proud to be British. Perhaps nothing epitomises that more than being a loyal Arsenal F.C. supporter for seventy years. The following pages chart his exceptional life story which can be summed up in his words:

> I volunteered for the British forces because I wanted to give something back to Britain for saving my life. Without it I would have perished in the Holocaust alongside my parents and other family members. I could have stayed in Australia or the Pioneer Corps where in either case life would have been easy, but I didn't. I wanted to fight the Germans. It was my duty.

CHAPTER 1

THE EARLY YEARS

Willy Hirschfeld was born in Bonn on 17 August 1920, one of twins, to Arthur and Regina Hirschfeld. His twin sister was named Dorothea. They had an older sister, Betty, and an older brother Manfred. Their parents Arthur and Regina married in 1909 in the local synagogue in Graudenz, West Prussia (now Poland). Arthur was born in Graudenz in 1879, Regina born in 1880 in the small village of Lessen, near Graudenz. Regina's family were Orthodox Jews but after her marriage she and Arthur kept a more relaxed Jewish household. Their first child Betty was born in 1910, and then Manfred in 1917. By 1912–3, Arthur Hirschfeld moved his family to Bonn, realising that things could get difficult for them as Jews if Graudenz became part of Poland, which it did in due course. He also managed to persuade his sister, known to Willy as Tante Hanna, to settle in Bonn along with some of Regina's family: her mother Flora Moses, and Henrietta and Marcus Moses. Life was good for the Hirschfelds in the early years in Bonn. Willy has only happy memories of early childhood before the Nazis shattered his youthful dreams and forced him to grow up faster than normal. His maternal grandmother, aunt and uncle lived in Bonn on Reuter Strasse. 'As a family,' he comments, 'we always looked after each other. We visited my grandmother, aunt and uncle every week to play cards. We had a good, happy family life.'

The Jews of Bonn were well-integrated into the life of the city; a university town on the river Rhine, which at that time had a population of just under 100,000. Around 1,100 were Jews. There were even Jewish professors at the university. Bonn was famous as the birthplace of composer Ludwig von Beethoven. Willy comments:

> Bonn is a beautiful place surrounded by lovely countryside, a friendly but sleepy city. During my childhood there were lots of Jewish stores around the city. The story goes that before Hitler came to power in Germany, he wanted to visit Bonn and stay in the famous Konigs Hof on the Rhine. It was the best hotel in the area. The owner knew that Hitler was anti-Semitic and refused him a room, saying that he had a lot of Jewish guests. Apparently, Hitler moved on to the next town on the Rhine called Bad Godesberg and stayed in the Hotel Dreesen. It was always felt that he never liked Bonn. I was pleased that on 29 November 1949, Bonn and not Berlin became the Bundes-haupstadt [capital] of West Germany. If it had been Berlin, it would have too many connections and memories for me of the Nazis.

Arthur Hirschfeld started out in 1913 as manager of a department store called Leonard Titz, the biggest store in Bonn. The following year, on 4 August 1914, war broke out, and Arthur was called up to fight in the German army. He served in an infantry regiment, seeing active service at the Battle of Verdun. He, like many of his generation, spoke very little about his experience of war. One postcard survives from this period, written by Arthur to his daughter Betty; it is dated 19 May 1917, just over three years before Willy and Dorothea were born. The postcard is a picture of Arthur with his regiment. Translated from German, it reads:

> Tomorrow off to Jülich. Packet from mother received. I hope that you are behaving yourself and good at school. I hope that you and dear mother are healthy and keep well. Kiss from father.

After the war, a Jewish organisation was formed in Bonn called *Jüdische Frontsoldaten*, a club for Jewish ex-servicemen who had fought for Germany in the 1914–18 war. It was more of a social club than a political organisation. Arthur Hirschfeld was a member and proud of it. Branches of the organisation sprang up all over the Rhineland. In 1923 Hirschfeld started his own business, opening a smart menswear shop in Gangolfstrasse, near the Minster. It was the year of Adolf Hitler's failed Putsch, when he and his supporters tried to take over the Bavarian government in Munich. Hitler was sentenced to five years imprisonment, during which time he wrote the first part of his infamous book *Mein Kampf* (published 1925). He was released after serving just nine months. He would have to wait another ten years to gain political power in Germany, and when it finally came it was swift and virtually absolute.

During the mid-1920s, Willy remembers playing in the yard at the back of his father's shop:

It had a single tree and my father's apprentice Willy Rebensburg, who was later one of the few good Germans of the Nazi period, made a swing for me. I used to play on it for hours. Sometimes my father had to go to Cologne on business and I always waited for him to return on that swing for hours! He always bought me back a chocolate Sarotti baby. I loved it. Willy Rebensburg sometimes took and collected us from kindergarten. He was not Jewish but always looked after us. He sometimes collected us from synagogue on Simchat Torah, the festival which celebrates the giving of the Law to Moses on Mount Sinai. We had to go around the synagogue with little flags. He made those flags for us with a Star of David.

The years of high inflation in Germany, especially in 1927, were exceptionally difficult for ordinary Germans. Willy Rebensburg stood by his boss through the tough times but at the end of 1929, Arthur Hirschfeld moved to premises in Wenzelgasse. With Arthur's agreement, Willy Rebensburg took over the old business on Gangolfstrasse.

Willy Hirschfeld, as he then was, has several fond memories of life back then. He vividly remembers finding 'inflation money' in the attic of their house and he and his twin sister Thea spent hours of fun playing with it. 'There were,' he says, 'several suitcases of it in the attic; all of no value any more. The large notes were worthless. That gives some idea of just how bad things were economically in Germany.' The effects of the First World War were visible all around. One of the requirements of the Versailles Treaty at the end of the war was that Germany could not maintain a military presence in the Rhineland. French and Moroccan troops, therefore, occupied the region until February 1926. Willy recalls that the French and Moroccan soldiers in and around Bonn 'were always exceptionally kind to us children and would often play with us. I always remember the day they marched out of Bonn and no longer occupied the city or Rhineland. These images made a great impression on me as a young boy.'

Until 1929, the Hirschfelds lived a comfortable life in a large three-storey house on Poppelsdorfer Allee, one of the most beautiful avenues in Bonn lined with chestnut trees on each side. They employed a cook and nanny. They were practising Jews and attended the synagogue in Bonn for the High Holy Day, Yom Kippur, Passover and some Friday and Saturday services. From 1927–30, Willy was educated in a non-Jewish primary school in Bonn. One of his most memorable school trips was to see the *Graf Zeppelin* airship which had landed at a small airfield at Hangelar, around 10km from Bonn: 'My sister and I both went with the school to see the *Graf Zeppelin*. It was an impressive sight and very exciting for a ten-year-old boy.' In 1931 Willy left primary school, the Münsterschule, and went to Stadt Gymnasium (grammar school). The high inflation of the late 1920s finally forced the family to move in 1930 from Poppelsdorfer Allee to an apartment on Lenné Strasse.

On 30 January 1933, Adolf Hitler came to power in Germany. The majority of Germans embraced their new leader and his policies, with his persuasive promises of employment at a time of high inflation and mass unemployment. He seemed to be injecting a yearned-for pride back into a nation which had been thoroughly humiliated after the First World War and had been forced to pay huge reparations. On 23 March 1933, Hitler's power was extended when the German parliament passed a bill enabling him to rule by decree. 'Now,' comments Willy, 'Hitler had made Germany a one-party Nazi state.' That power was to have terrible consequences for the Jews of Europe, beginning gradually with their marginalisation from public life and leading ultimately to mass murder in the concentration camps. Within a few years, it became more than just denying Jews and other groups of their civil liberties. The evil dictatorship's aim turned to ways of ridding first Germany, and then all Nazi-occupied land, of its Jewish population altogether. Just six years later, Hitler's aggression towards Germany's neighbours would lead Europe into another world war. And his 'Final Solution' to the 'Jewish problem' would lead to the annihilation in the gas chambers of six million Jews, plus five million others (gypsies, homosexuals, disabled people). Over a period of time, Bonn could not escape the changes which the Nazi regime imposed on Germany. Certain streets and squares were renamed, for example Friedensplatz became Adolf-Hitler Platz. (These names were restored after the war.) Nazi flags hung from buildings in the main street and gradually Jewish shops disappeared. On 1 April 1933 the Nazis boycotted Jewish shops and businesses in Germany. Signs appeared on Jewish shops saying, for example: 'This is a Jewish shop. You are not allowed to shop here.' On non-Jewish shops, signs read '*Juden sind unerwünscht*' (Jews not allowed here). The same signs appeared on public swimming pools, at dentists, doctors and cinemas. Hitler's rise to power affected Arthur Hirschfeld's business, as it did many Jews. Eventually, he had to give up his shop because Jewish businesses were boycotted or taken away by the Nazis. Willy vividly remembers the regime change in Germany:

I remember Hitler coming to power. I was twelve and a half years old. We were living in Lenné Strasse at the time. The Germans started marching through the streets of Bonn with fire torches. We were in our bedroom one night when I was awoken by German SA (Brown Shirts) marching in their hundreds past our house and down the streets. They were singing the famous *Horst Wessel* marching song. This happened in the middle of the night. I didn't realise at that time just how bad it would be for us. My parents knew – they saw the writing on the wall and it turned my mother into a very nervous person. They realised it signalled trouble for the Jews of Germany and that would include us. Bonn was nearer to France and Belgium than Berlin, and therefore it took Bonn longer to become anti-Semitic than elsewhere in Germany. The anti-Jewish measures and anti-Semitic attacks didn't start immediately for us. A few Jewish shops still traded in Bonn until 1938 and Jewish children could still attend Aryan schools until 1934–5. But I did notice an immediate difference at school. The Germans love uniforms and as soon as Hitler came to power, all my non-Jewish friends became members of the Hitler Youth (Hitlerjugend). They wore a special uniform which marked them out as different from us. They strutted around with their brown shirts, brown trousers, and swastika armbands. They were brainwashed with the new Nazi ideology and propaganda. Consequently I lost school friends at this time because non-Jewish children were no longer allowed to play with Jewish boys in the school and that included me. For the first time in my life, I was made to feel different, inferior, and that experience was true for the other Jewish boys in my school.

On 7 April 1933 a law was passed in Germany prohibiting Jews from practising in the legal profession. Just over a month later, on 10 May, Joseph Goebbels, the Nazi Minister of Propaganda, ordered the burning of 'undesirable' books of leading Jewish intellectuals, such as Karl Marx and Sigmund Freud. In Berlin's university square, academics and students gathered to begin an action that would see the burning of some 20,000 books. Such was the brainwashing of the German people that some of the younger generation had no knowledge of what they were burning, having never read the books being thrown into the flames. Willy witnessed the book-burning in Bonn:

> I remember walking on my way home to Lenné Strasse that day and seeing Brown Shirts and Hitler Youth throwing books onto a large bonfire. At that point, I didn't know what was going on or that it was Jewish books they were burning. It didn't take me long to find out and it seemed almost unbelievable to me that this was what they had done.

Later that summer in August 1933, Willy celebrated his bar mitzvah in the synagogue in Bonn. It was a special time for him and religiously marked his transition into manhood. During the service, he was called up to read from the scroll of the Torah in Hebrew.

> It is quite an occasion for a boy of thirteen. The whole community was rejoicing that, according to our religion, I was entering life as a male adult. I had the whole Jewish community celebrating with me that day. After the bar mitzvah, we had open house for tea and cake. There were no lavish presents in those days. I received a wrist watch from my elder sister Betty; a propelling pencil, and some books. Little did we know just how bad it would get for the Jews of Germany, including my community in Bonn. Our lives would soon be disrupted by the Nazi regime, our civil liberties denied bit by bit.

A glimpse of the brutality which lay ahead was witnessed by Willy just days before his bar mitzvah. He was making his way home from school, the Stadt Gymnasium, when he saw his best friend lying dead in the street. Karl Heinz Grunewald was Jewish and had happened to make a nasty remark about a Hitler Youth. He was immediately shot. Willy recalls the injustice, saying: 'The fellow who killed my friend Karl was honoured by the Nazis afterwards.' And that was not the only brutality that Willy remembers. A local Jewish butcher was beaten by the SS and put in one of his freezers. Although he was rescued, he subsequently died. Willy comments:

> It was a frightening time for us. Such acts against Jews were becoming a daily reality. We could no longer mix with Aryans. Gradually some of our Jewish friends managed to emigrate to USA, South America and England.

On 2 August 1934 Germany's President Hindenburg died at the age of eighty-six, paving the way for Adolf Hitler to grasp a tighter hold on power. Hitler was proclaimed 'Führer and Reichskanzler' (Chancellor). The situation could only get worse for Germany's Jews. Under the Treaty of Versailles, which had set out terms for peace at the end of the First World War, Germany was forbidden to rearm or have more than 100,000 in the armed forces. With the death of Hindenburg, Hitler's power was absolute. He began to rearm the nation in contravention of the terms of the Treaty of Versailles. By the following year he had formed the Luftwaffe, the German air force, and introduced conscription for men between eighteen and forty-five. That same year, 1934, Willy's education, and that of his twin sister Thea, was affected when they were not allowed to attend a state school anymore:

> Everyday life was almost normal for us in the early days of Hitler, except at school where Jewish children had to sit in the back row of the classroom and were completely ignored. I was the lead gymnast in my class, but now I lost that role for being Jewish. This was worrying for me. Things gradually got worse for us. After school, I often had fights with the son of the man who ran the local Nazi newspaper *Westdeutcher Beachter* [West German Observer]. His office was right opposite our school. I didn't know then how risky it was for a Jewish boy to fight with a non-Jew. It would only be a matter of months later and I would have paid with my life for it. The fights went on until 1934 when I was thrown out of school for being Jewish. My teacher told me that 'we don't wish to have you here anymore'. That applied to all Jewish pupils. We could not really relax until we went to a Jewish school.

From 1934, Jewish children of Bonn found themselves without any means of education. A Jewish school was hurriedly established in a house belonging to the Jewish Masonic Lodge. Children were placed in two classes according to age: one for ages six to ten, the other for over tens. They were taught basic subjects: mathematics, English, drama, history and Jewish history. It became more like a social community than a school.

> For us Jewish children, we were lucky that our teacher was first class and very dedicated. With all that was going on in Germany, we talked about the future. We knew that it would be the end of us if we did not emigrate. The school prepared us for emigration and tried to teach us a profession or trade. We learnt the English and French languages. Everything was done under threat. It was a vulnerable situation for us. We lived completely in fear. But it was not easy to get out of Germany. One could not just leave the

country and go anywhere you chose. You needed a visa, a working permit and money. Most countries had strict quotas for entry, and that included Britain. You really needed relatives living abroad who could organise it.

In 1934/5 an offshoot of the *Jüdische Frontsoldaten* club for Jewish ex-servicemen formed a sports club for Jewish children who were excluded from public sports activities. Willy jumped at the opportunity to play in the junior football team. There was also a senior football team and ladies handball team. They were able to compete against other Jewish groups in the Rhineland. As Willy says, 'It was one of the few privileges for us at that time. The nearer we got to 1938 even the sports stopped because we were forbidden to have Jewish-only football teams. I was no longer able to play the sport which was my life's passion.'

There was worse news for Germany's Jews when, in the summer of 1935, Hitler passed the Nuremberg Laws, effectively rendering Jews outcast from all remaining aspects of public life. By law, Jews were no longer allowed to buy goods from Aryan shops or have Aryan servants. They were not permitted to travel on trams or buses, or use public swimming pools or parks. Teaching Hebrew was forbidden and all Jewish passports were withdrawn to be stamped with a red J for *Juden*. Willy recalls:

> The degradation of Jews was as good as complete. We had no rights in Germany and were seen as people of 'impure blood'. We were no longer German citizens, only 'subjects' – we Jews whose fathers had proudly fought for Germany in the First World War. We were singled out as inferior to other Germans. Later that same year, in November 1935, no Jew in Germany was allowed to hold any public office, nor to vote, or marry a non-Jew. When you realise that the State is out to get you, it is a terrible thing. You are made to feel guilty about every breath of air you breathe. We tried to carry on a normal life in abnormal circumstances. My parents tried to shelter us as much as possible, and my mother in particular worried about our safety. She could never relax until we were safely home each night.

In July 1936 a further violation of the Treaty of Versailles occurred when Hitler ordered troops to enter the Rhineland. The area had been declared a de-militarised zone under the Treaty. The occupation included Bonn. Willy remembers the day soldiers entered the city:

My sister Thea and I were going through Bonn's main park the Hofgarten. That day the German Reichwehr [army] came on horseback with drums beating and marched with a band through the park. I was terribly impressed by the size of it all. Seeing all the men on horseback in their impressive uniforms was not lost on me as a young lad, but little did I realise the full implications. Thereafter they were a daily reality in the area with SS and Brown Shirts. It wasn't the army that was a threat to us Jews; it was the SS, SA and Gestapo that were after us.

In 1936 Arthur Hirschfeld lost his business to the Nazis. Dire circumstances forced all of the Hirschfeld children, including Willy, to seek work to feed the family. At that time, work could only be found with other Jewish businesses or employers.

After father lost the shop, it was difficult to get work. An old Jewish friend of his had a wholesale shop in textiles; he gave my father linen and towels in a suitcase to go out and sell. My father travelled by bus or train into the countryside to sell to farmers and villages where there were no proper shops. As soon as he got money, he bought new goods. But this didn't last long because no one wanted to buy from Jews. We fell on very hard times. My elder sister Betty earned some money locally in Jewish shops still functioning. My brother Manfred worked for a wood merchant and sister Thea worked in a sweet shop. We children earned a little to help the family survive. My father then played cards secretly to get money. I remember my mother would turn up at the place where he played cards at midday. Sometimes he could give her the winnings to buy food. My mother was an amazing person. She originally came from a wealthy background, so life was hard for her now. She became very nervous. She was always worried about us children during the Nazi period. She was remarkable because she never complained about having to change her lifestyle and adapt to a life of poverty. She coped very well with our financial position under Hitler. She kept the family together.

In April 1936 Willy took up employment as an apprentice at a metal-smelting company called Metalhuttenwerke Herz & Co., which belonged to a Jewish company in Siegburg, a few miles east of Bonn. His first job there involved sorting scrap metal. Each day he travelled the short train journey to work. The Jewish owner, Mr Herz, fled Germany in 1937 for Belgium and then England, after his business was confiscated by the Nazis. Willy lost touch with him for a couple of years, but Herz was to be pivotal in getting Willy out of Germany in 1939. With the business now in new hands, the company changed its name to MIRUS, and Willy was allowed to continue working there. He comments:

> In all fairness the new owner was not a Nazi. In fact he was a very religious Catholic man and kept me on as an employee. I was lucky to have a job at that time and earn money. This was vital because my father couldn't get a job anymore and we had to feed the family somehow.

But the situation in Bonn worsened for the Hirschfeld family. Lack of sufficient income forced them to move from Lenné Strasse to Liszt Strasse where they had only two rooms. They stayed there for about four months before renting a small place in Dorotheen Strasse in the north of Bonn.

> We only stayed in Liszt Strasse for such a short time because Jews were no longer able to live in certain districts of Bonn. We had to move out to poorer areas, but by now it had become really difficult for Jews to find any accommodation. Non-Jews were unwilling to rent even a room to us. The situation became quite desperate for many Jewish families in Bonn. We were fortunate enough to find someone who would rent us a small flat in Dorotheen Strasse.

Some of Willy's friends were able to emigrate, but emigration was not possible for the Hirschfelds at this time because they did not have the financial means to leave Germany, nor a guarantor abroad to get them out:

Throughout 1936 and 1937 we managed to live as best we could. It was a frightening time because you never knew when we might be targeted by the Gestapo or SS. Our freedom was restricted. We couldn't go to certain public places, like parks or swimming baths. We were made to feel second-class citizens by the state. We constantly feared for the future.

On 17 November 1937, Willy's grandmother Flora Moses died at the age of eighty-seven. It was the first death for the family: 'In spite of her age, it was a shock for me when she died. I adored my grandmother and felt the loss deeply. We attended her funeral. I was seventeen at the time. It was a very sad day. She is buried in the Jewish cemetery in Bonn.' Tragedy was to strike the family again the following year when Willy's eldest sister Betty died on 17 July 1938 in a hospital in Cologne after a short mysterious illness. She was twenty-eight years old.

It was a terrible time for the family. Betty was taken ill so suddenly and the next thing we knew she had died. In those days you never talked about illness and so we didn't really know what she had died of. The circumstances surrounding her death were all very odd. After the Second World War, I tried to find out from official German records how she died, but could never get a normal answer. All I could get is confirmation that she had died but they have no trace of the cause of death. I have always believed that something happened that has been covered up. She had been ill for only a short time, even so, why is there no record of the cause of death? The whole family naturally attended her funeral. It was a grim day for us. It was a terrible thing to bury one's sister at such a young age. My mother was heartbroken. Betty was already engaged to be married and was due to emigrate to Holland. My only consolation when I think of her today is that at least she was spared the Holocaust. She is also buried in the Jewish cemetery in Bonn. I visit her grave and that of my grandmother each year when I go back to Bonn.

It was just a couple of months after his sister's funeral that Willy and his family were caught up in unimaginable events. The precarious situation for Jews like Willy was about to escalate. All seemed hopeful when, from 22–24 September 1938, British Prime Minister Neville Chamberlain stayed at the Petersberg Hotel on the banks of the Rhine not far from Bonn. He had flown to Germany for face-to-face talks with Adolf Hitler. During their conference, Hitler stayed in the Hotel Dreesen, his favourite hotel nearby. The two leaders met at the Petersberg Hotel to discuss the crisis over the Sudetenland. At the end of the month, on 30 September, they signed the Munich Agreement. Chamberlain returned to Britain promising 'peace in our time'. Britain was not ready for another war; the memories of the horrors of the First World War and the loss of millions of lives still deeply affected the nation.

While Chamberlain returned from Germany with renewed optimism, it was only a matter of weeks before the situation for Europe's Jews dramatically deteriorated. At the end of October 1938, Hitler ordered the deportation of all Polish Jews from Germany to Zbuczyn, a border town in no-man's-land between Germany and Poland. This policy was soon to have devastating consequences for the Jews of Germany and Austria. Willy reflects:

All Polish Jews had to leave Bonn, and that included quite a few of my own friends. I never saw any of them again. I have vivid memories of the Polish Jews in our city being herded together and taken away. Little could we know then that ten days later, Europe's Jews would suffer horrifically at the hands of the Nazis on *Kristallnacht*, the Night of Broken Glass. It so happened that that night would change my life forever.

CHAPTER 2

DACHAU CONCENTRATION CAMP

On 7 November 1938 German diplomat Ernst vom Rath was shot in Paris by Polish Jew Herschel Grynszpan in retaliation for the deportation of his family to Zbuczyn. Rath was in a critical condition in a French hospital. The Jews of Germany and Austria were to pay a heavy price for Grynszpan's action. They could not possibly have foreseen the full-scale retaliation that would be exacted on them by the Nazis for the action of a single student. Retribution came two days later. On 9 November vom Rath died from his wounds. That day also happened to be the fifteenth anniversary of Hitler's failed putsch (coup) in Munich in 1923. The death of vom Rath was the excuse Hitler was waiting for to incite an outburst of violence against the Jews. His propaganda minister Joseph Goebbels ordered a violent progrom against the Jews of Germany and Austria; attacks which the State falsely claimed were random and not orchestrated in advance. During the day of 9 November and the night of the 10th, the Nazis unleashed *Kristallnacht*, the Night of Broken Glass. In towns, villages and cities across Germany and Austria, stormtroopers smashed the windows of Jewish businesses, looted Jewish shops and the buildings torched. Synagogues were set on fire, and with them, the scrolls of the Torah – the first five books of Moses. Throughout Germany and Austria over a thousand synagogues were destroyed that night, many becoming burnt-out shells of their former glory. Terror gripped the Jewish inhabitants who remained behind closed doors for fear of their lives. The destruction was as yet unparalleled since Hitler had come to power in Germany five years earlier. In total, nearly 100 Jews were killed and 25,000 arrested and sent to concentration camps. That terrifying night was an ominous sign of worse to come for Europe's Jews. If they were ever in doubt about Hitler's power to last as Chancellor of Germany-Austria, the actions that night proved them wrong. He had an unprecedented hold on power and had singled them out, although the full policy of the Final Solution was not formalised until 1942.

On the morning of 10 November, Willy walked as usual to the railway station for the thirty-minute train journey to work. En route he saw several Jewish shops with their windows smashed in and glass littering the pavements. Some premises were still on fire and others completely looted. He comments:

> Our synagogue was not very far from the station. From there I could see smoke and I noticed that our synagogue was on fire. It was an awful thing to see. No attempt was made to put out the fire still raging. The fire brigade was just interested in making sure the houses either side were not affected. The synagogue was burned out completely that night, the SS and police made sure of that. I was very distressed by this, but still I decided to carry on to the factory. I was very worried. I did not know if I should carry on to the factory or whether I should go back home. I decided to go to work as usual. At the factory they all knew I was Jewish, but this didn't affect my relationship with the other workers because I didn't look Jewish and that helped a lot.

When Willy arrived at the factory gates the manager, who was Italian, told him there were going to be problems. He was concerned about the turn of events and suggested that Willy should be hidden somewhere in the factory. It was proposed to hide him in one of the big oil furnaces which were not being used at that time. Willy's response was 'don't be silly.' He had not considered himself personally at risk. But it was too late. At that moment two Gestapo officers, one in SS uniform and another in a long leather coat, marched in:

> They asked me: 'Are you Willy Hirschfeld?'
>
> I replied, 'Yes, I am.'
>
> They said, 'You have to come with us. You are being arrested.'
>
> My manager, who was an Italian, argued with the Gestapo not to take me away because my skills were vital for the specialist work in the factory. The factory made metal ingots which were blocks of differing mixes of metal: brass, aluminium, zinc or copper. It was a skill to get this mix right and I was one of the few workers who could. These ingots were needed for German industry. I vividly remember the manager really protesting at my impending arrest. He took a risk arguing with the Gestapo. They just told him, 'Never mind what he can do, he is a Jew and we need to take him.' All argument fell on deaf ears.

Willy was promptly taken to an unknown Gestapo headquarters, somewhere he did not recognise. He was then interrogated about the whereabouts of his former boss Mr Herz, of whom he knew nothing. He was punched several times during the interrogation. From there he was driven by car to a high security prison in Cologne. He was interrogated again and initially kept in isolation.

> I was thrown into a small, dingy cell with no windows. There was only a wooden bed and a bucket for urinating. It was an extremely grim and frightening experience especially when the door was slammed and locked. It was dreadful. I was only eighteen at the time. Questions raced through my mind – why had I been arrested? What had I done? I had never been in prison before. It was the worst thing that could happen to me because I hadn't done anything wrong. There was huge uncertainty about what would happen to me. We all knew about Nazi brutality – we had lived under the regime for five years at that point. Would I be shot? Or released? What was coming next? That weighed heavily on my mind and was extremely frightening.

Willy was kept in the cell on his own for a few days. Then, one day, he heard lots of shouting. He realised that more people had arrived in the prison. He heard everything that was going on in the corridor outside his cell:

> The prison became very overcrowded with Jewish men. I recall that at least two other Jewish men were thrown into my cell. It was dreadful conditions and now we had to sleep on the floor. We had no idea what was going to happen to any of us. I was then interrogated by the Gestapo and suffered some brutality. They asked me about things of which I knew nothing. They asked lots of questions about my former Jewish boss Mr Herz, but I didn't have a clue of his whereabouts. I couldn't honestly tell them anything. I was threatened and beaten.

The following day the prison guard asked Willy if he would be prepared to do some work in the prison. He volunteered, relieved to spend some time out of the cell. Little did he realise what kind of work it would be. His job was to empty all the overflowing buckets of urine. He says: 'It was a dreadful job on the one hand, but in a strange way, I was glad to be doing something.'

Five days later, on 15 November, Willy and hundreds of other men were loaded onto a cattle-train during the night for an unknown destination. He feared the worst.

> We were marched in line out of Cologne prison, about 200 or 300 of us, and taken to a railway station. It was night time. I was aware that the train was full of prisoners like me. We were shunted into cattle trucks with no seats in them. There were no windows and we couldn't see what was going on. All we could hear was shouting and screaming. I was one of the youngest men in my wagon. I cannot recall having any food or drink. After a long journey, about five or six hours, we arrived at our destination. It was around 3 a.m. I heard shouting and dogs barking. The doors were opened; there were searchlights and SS officers everywhere. We were shunted out of the train with SS men on either side with rifles. Those of us who did not get out quick enough were hit by the butt of their

rifles. I got hit on the head and fell down, but I could take it. I was young and able to get up. Other older men fell down, couldn't get up, and were beaten further. I suspected we were going somewhere dreadful, but I did not know exactly where. As soon as the searchlight went on, I read clearly the words over the gate: *Arbeit Macht Frei* [work makes you free]. And I knew then that we were in a concentration camp.

Willy and fellow inmates had arrived at Dachau concentration camp, 7km north-west of Munich. The camp had been opened in March 1933 as the first of Hitler's concentration camps meant for opponents of the Nazis. It was intended to act as a deterrent; to scare the German people into submission to Nazi rule. The commandant, Theodor Eicke, ran a brutal regime with squads of SS Death's Head units. Until its liberation in April 1945, over 200,000 prisoners were incarcerated in the camp. Officially, at least 30,000 died there, although the real figure is probably higher since many deaths went unrecorded. Until 1938, most of those held there were political prisoners of the state, communists and Social Democrats. According to those who had arrested them, they had been taken there 'for their own protection'.

By the time Willy arrived in November 1938, the camp was already holding several thousand inmates, but numbers swelled after *Kristallnacht*, with over 10,000 German Jews alone imprisoned in Dachau. Soon other groups joined them: gypsies, homosexuals, clergymen who were anti-Nazi and Jehovah's Witnesses. Several of the Jewish prisoners from November 1938 were released at the beginning of 1939 if they had a valid visa and declared it their intention to leave the country immediately. But many of those who were released first, were captured again if they did not manage to escape from Germany in time. They were deported to the ghettos and extermination camps in Eastern Europe. Willy's entry into the camp was recorded in the *Zugangsbücher* (intake ledger book) under the name Wilhelm Hirschfeld. His incarceration in Dachau on 15 November 1938 was the beginning of a four-month-long nightmare. He recalls:

At the entrance we had to hand over all our belongings which were put into a sack with our names and number on it. I was number 28411.

We now had no legal rights. We were totally at the mercy of the guards. We were then driven like cattle onto the parade ground. We all had to undress. It was the middle of winter. We stood naked in the parade ground whilst we were hosed down with ice cold water. Eventually we were given the standard concentration camp clothing: blue and white striped pyjamas and our heads were shaven.

The camp was surrounded by a barbed-wire electric fence with watch-towers, and a moat. Inside the complex there were lines of huts, a parade ground and disinfectant hut for clothing. The camp had a prison or 'bunker', prison yard and wall where many prisoners were shot. Prisoners who were being admitted to the camp for a second time suffered harsher conditions and were isolated from other inmates in three barrack huts. Willy was taken to hut 20 which became his accommodation for the duration of his incarceration. Each hut was desperately overcrowded, with rows upon rows of wooden bunks three levels high. There were no mattresses, only straw and a blanket for bedding; nor were there any toilets, just holes in the ground. The camp was run on a strict daily routine. The first roll-call was at 5 a.m. on the main parade ground. Breakfast was at 5.30 a.m. which was followed by work until lunchtime. Work began again at 1 p.m. until 6.30 p.m. or dusk. Final roll-call was at 7 p.m. Between 7 p.m. and 9 p.m. when lights went out, the men were confined to their huts. It was the first time that Willy had come into contact with Austrian Jews. 'There were quite a few of them in my hut,' he recalls. 'There was always a self-imposed division between Austrians and Germans; but I always got on very well with them.' The youngest members of each hut were sent to the kitchen to collect the food for the others. On the first morning, Willy and another inmate were asked to fetch the large cauldron of coffee for their hut. In reality, the 'coffee' was nothing more than hot brown water:

The heavy metal cauldron had two handles which needed two of us to carry, which I did with another inmate. I didn't realise it was full of hot 'coffee'. We were ordered to run across the camp, instead of walk. The hot coffee went all over our hands. I tried to avoid being asked to do this again because I had burnt my hands quite badly. Our breakfast consisted of black stale bread and watery coffee. That was all we had to eat until midday. The working day began at 6 a.m. Lunch was at 12 noon. Again, someone had to collect our food which was transported to the huts in cauldrons with either coffee, potatoes or 'meat'. When I had to do it again, I was wiser this time and picked up the potatoes. Our diet consisted solely of potatoes, not peeled, with a kind of goulash which later we found out was whale meat. The food was terrible but it kept us going.

The winter of 1938 was terribly cold, with snow on the ground making conditions unbearably harsh. Willy was consigned to a labour team that spent hours each day clearing snow from the camp. He was confronted with Nazi brutality on a daily basis:

It was a dreadful place. I saw lots of things happen. Elderly people who couldn't cope with life in the camp walked into the electric wire that surrounded the camp. In that way they took their own life before the Nazis did. People were shot just because they did not do as they were ordered by the guards. Very often, early in the morning before roll-call, we noticed some of our inmates lying dead on the ground because they had thrown themselves at the electric wire or had been killed by a guard. At night time, the camp had a terrible eerie feeling.

It was essential that every man was present at each roll-call, otherwise the consequences were appalling. Willy recalls:

One of the roll-calls stays in my mind. It was found that one man was missing and we were forced to stand in blocks of a hundred inmates on the parade ground until he was found. We stood for at least two days and two nights in the bitter November cold, a total of between 48–60 hours with no respite. We always made sure that the younger ones were on the outside to protect the elderly inmates from the cold. At least 40–50 people died on the parade ground during this incident. They just fell to the ground and we were not allowed to help them. That first night we saw dead bodies being carried away on a horse-drawn cart. It was a terrible sight that always lives with me. The missing man was eventually found hidden in a toilet. We can only guess what happened to him. One of my friends nearly collapsed and I held him for about half an hour. An SS man came over to me and told me to drop him. They took him away. I don't know what happened to him. I was frightened that I would be punished for helping him. We knew that the penalty was twenty-five lashes and that it was virtually impossible to survive the lashes. By some act of fate, the guard forgot about what I had done for my friend and I was never punished, but for days I feared that punishment was imminent. Living under that threat was frightening. I also knew that once you had marks on your body, or any physical sign of brutality, you would never be released from the camp. We always lived in hope that one day we would be freed. I survived that terrifying ordeal, probably because I was young and fit.

Punishment in the camp was severe, even for minor offences: A penalty of eight days' detention and twenty-five strokes for anyone making a joke or jeering remarks at an SS officer, or failing to salute at the appropriate time; a penalty of fourteen days' detention for anyone entering or leaving a hut or building other than through the prescribed entrance (i.e. not through windows) or smoking in the living quarters; a penalty of twenty-one days' detention for anyone damaging property of the State; and a penalty of forty-two days' detention and prolonged solitary confinement for anyone collecting money in the camp, communicating anything to a priest other than spiritual matters or giving the priests letters to smuggle out of the camp; and also for those who vilify the emblem of the State or those who wear it. Solitary confinement meant a period of having only water and dry bread and a hard bed to sleep on. Hot food would only be given every four days. Hard physical labour was enforced, especially dirty work carried out under strict surveillance by camp guards. The slightest gossip between inmates, especially if a small group had formed, could be construed as subversive activity or provocative behaviour. The penalty for that laid down in the camp's penal code was death:'any person ... will be hanged as a subversive instigator under the terms of the revolutionary law.' Willy lived in constant fear, watching his every step, movement and word spoken. He remembers:

> The fear that was instilled into us was chilling. We were often too frightened to talk to each other. As soon as SS men entered the hut, the nearest person had to call *Achtung* [watch out!]. We all had to stand to attention. To this day I hate the word *Achtung* because of all the images it conjures up for me. I never use it when speaking German. I remember an occasion when one of our inmates didn't stand to attention. It was a young Jewish man of about thirty. When the SS asked him why he didn't stand still, he said, 'I don't stand up for an SS man.' He took his pistol out and shot him. We were told 'that will teach you all a lesson'. Very often, we heard shots during the nights because inmates were not allowed to leave the huts once lights were out. We never talked to each other about what happened. We all knew the reality. We presumed someone had tried to escape and was shot.

In the overcrowded huts where the men slept, they were required to hang their towel next to their bed. The towel was no more than a scrappy piece of rag, but if it was not neatly folded they were beaten by one of the guards. Each hut had one man in charge called a Capo, usually a long-term political prisoner; a communist. They had a fearsome reputation for widespread brutality amongst the inmates. Willy experienced no such behaviour. He was fortunate that his Capo befriended him. The Capo had studied calligraphy and sometimes, in the evening, he would call Willy into his tiny room where he had a table, and tried to teach him calligraphy and sign-writing. It kept Willy's mind off the terrible things that were happening in the camp. He also allocated Willy the task of cleaning the windows of the hut which meant some respite from long hours shovelling snow across the camp. The windows had to be cleaned to perfection with ice cold water using old newspaper as a cloth – one spot of dirt left on the windows and he faced a beating.

The concentration camp was full of Jewish professionals: doctors, dentists, architects and businessmen. The elderly men amongst them had served in the German army in the First World War and could not comprehend why they were being imprisoned in a concentration camp.

Their service in the war seemed to count for nothing. A couple of months later they were amongst the first to be released and that gave Willy and other inmates hope that they would be next. He says, 'it gave us strength to keep going and bear the grim conditions.'

Eventually, for a while, the huts had fewer inmates and the men were given individual bunk beds which was much better than communal bunks. Willy was given a bunk under the window, but 'during the night I was conscious that you mustn't get up and your shadow be seen through the window. The SS guards would wonder why you were awake and think you were trying to escape.' If any inmate was unwell, it was not advisable to go to the medical hut because, as Willy was told: 'You won't come back.' People died in those medical centres. One particular day he had terrible toothache and feared going to the camp doctor:

> We had no toothbrushes in the concentration camp. There was nothing
> I could do to relieve the pain. Fortunately we had a Jewish dentist in my
> hut. My Capo got him an ordinary pair of pliers, brought ice from outside
> and packed it onto my face which froze it and they pulled out my tooth.

Back in Bonn, it was an anxious period for Willy's family while they tried to establish his whereabouts. They knew he had been arrested at the factory because one of his cousins who also worked there had witnessed the events. She came back and told his parents, but no one knew where he was being held. Eventually his parents were informed that he was in Dachau concentration camp. Willy was the only member of his family to have been arrested on *Kristallnacht*.

Some time later Willy was permitted to send a standard postcard from the camp to his parents: 'The postcard was censored and we could only say that we were being well looked after.' Family and friends then worked tirelessly to secure Willy's release.

The only way out of the camp was to produce papers for emigration. Willy's parents began to organise the necessary paperwork, such as copies of his birth certificate and forms to prove that he owed no taxes or bills to the government. They tried to buy him a train ticket to Shanghai via Russia which would have cost 1,000 marks, but ultimately they could not find the money. They were also advised that going across Russia would be unwise and dangerous. They finally got in touch with Willy's former boss Mr Herz who had already emigrated to England. He secured an agricultural permit for Willy to come to England to work on a farm, with the aim of him later settling in Palestine. Willy comments: 'Somehow I had a notion, because people *were* leaving, that my time would come soon and my hopes were very high.' Then one day, before official notification was given, Willy heard from his Capo that he was due for release very soon. He told Willy that papers were on their way to secure his exit. Willy then received a letter from his parents reassuring him that something would happen shortly. That gave him further hope. He waited anxiously for his release, but the whole visa process was delayed by a couple of weeks because his permit was sent to a Willy Hirschfeld in Berlin, not Bonn. The mistake was noticed and the permit was finally passed on to his parents. They then presented the papers to the Gestapo in Bonn and the relevant documents for Willy's release from Dachau were signed.

Once the paperwork had come through, and before he could leave the camp, Willy had to pass a medical examination from the camp doctor. It was a difficult time because a single mark, blemish or sign of Nazi brutality on his body and he could not be freed. The Nazi authorities made every attempt to hide from the outside world the ill-treatment of the inmates, even if that meant never granting their release. Those due for release had to be signed out as completely fit and healthy. In Willy's case, he had developed frostbite on one of his toes from standing in the winter cold, something which caused great concern because he knew it could prevent him from being allowed to leave. Once again, his Capo was of help and forewarned him, advising him how he could do something about his toe. A fellow Jewish inmate, a doctor, came to his rescue.

We had a Jewish doctor in our hut who tried to sort out my toe. The best he could do was to rub earth on it to cover up the redness. When it came to my medical, I was checked over and no one noticed my toe. The doctor had camouflaged it very well. If the camp medical officer had noticed my toe, I would not have been released until it was better. It was thanks to the Capo that I was given sufficient warning.

It was April 1939 and the time had come for Willy's release. Even now the situation was tense; even at the last minute, freedom was not assured.

> When I came to be released, the SS officer asked me if I had any money to pay for my fare home. Of course I had no money whatsoever. He replied, 'then you can't go. We are not paying.' To my amazement a fellow Jewish inmate, who was being released at the same time, looked up and said, 'I am a solicitor in Cologne. I'll pay for your fare.' And he did. But for him, I would have remained in the camp.

Willy was to experience one further act of kindness just moments before his release. This time it came unexpectedly from a camp guard. He handed in his camp clothing and received his belongings in return. He was required to sign a form to say that he had been very well treated. He was then told that he could purchase food for the journey home from the SS canteen:

> I stood in the corner waiting. The SS officer said, 'Why aren't you queue-ing up for something to eat?' I replied, 'I haven't got any money.' He took me to the front of the queue and asked me what I would like. He then proceeded to pay for my food. It was an incredible experience. It was the only act of kindness from an SS officer in four months.

Willy had to sign a pledge never to talk about what had happened or what he had seen in the camp. He was left under no illusion that if he did, he would be re-arrested and returned to the camp, never to be released under any circumstances. He duly signed the form.

The moment Willy had waited for, hoped for, for four terrifying months had finally arrived. He walked through the gates to freedom, passing under the words which had greeted his arrival and which would haunt him for decades: *Arbeit macht frei*. He comments, 'Finally I could say goodbye to Dachau concentration camp.' As he stepped onto the train he was a shadow of his former self; head shaven, pale, terribly thin and gaunt. The Nazis had temporarily added twenty years to his face.

As the train passed through Munich station, members of the local Jewish community were waiting for concentration camp survivors on the platform. Willy remembers it vividly:

> I still had a shaven head. Local Jews were waiting to hand out trilby hats to hide our identity as having come from a concentration camp. I was given one because they didn't want me to be recognised as a former inmate of a camp. It gave us dignity after our terrible incarceration in Dachau.

This remarkable gesture gave him and other newly released men the confidence to face the outside world, a world which since Willy's arrest four months earlier had moved closer to war. On 15 March 1939 Hitler had occupied Czechoslovakia. Britain, the place where Willy was destined to emigrate within the month, was trying to avoid another world war. Just twenty-one years after the end of the First World War, the country was not prepared for more bloodshed. Prime Minister Neville Chamberlain sought ways to appease Hitler and avert another slaughter on the fields of Europe.

Willy finally arrived in Bonn in the early hours of the morning. He did not dare ring the doorbell of his home because his parents would fear it was a Gestapo raid. He waited an hour before the long-awaited reunion. It was, he says, 'impossible to describe'. Family and friends commented how generally sad and degraded he looked in spite of being overjoyed to be home. His mother, who had become a very nervous person throughout all this, tried to feed him up. Willy in turn noticed the changes at home. By now his parents had very little money, having been virtually stripped of all they had through lack of business and proper employment.

Physically and emotionally exhausted from his long ordeal, Willy proceeded to sleep solidly for two days. There is a touching story about this time which links back to Willy's childhood. Every Christmas his mother used to prepare a *bunter-teller*, a basket filled with lots of treats like little pieces of marzipan, chocolate, nuts, figs, an orange and an apple. Each of the children got an identical *bunter-teller*.

> Our mother's *bunter-tellers* were the highlight of the year for us children. We loved it. The Christmas of 1938, I was in Dachau. My mother always

held on to the firm hope that one day I would be released. That Christmas she still made me a *bunter-teller* and kept it all those months for me. It was the first thing she gave me when I returned home in April 1939. It was one of the gestures I shall never forget.

There was a huge sense of relief that Willy was now safe, but time was running out. He had to leave the country within three weeks or face deportation back to a concentration camp. He made final preparations for his emigration to England. The new boss at the factory where Willy had worked discovered that he had come home, and in spite of the difficulties of employing a Jew, offered him employment until he emigrated: 'I did go back to work for him to earn some money to help my parents to survive. I felt alright going back to work after the terrible things that had happened to me.' Those memories of Dachau continued to haunt Willy for decades to come. Unable to speak about the experience, he carried the burden of memories locked in a wall of silence. When he eventually opened up years later, one question was repeatedly asked of him: 'Why didn't you try to escape from Dachau?'

He responds:

It was impossible. The camp itself was surrounded by a moat, an electric barbed-wire fence and wall with watchtowers manned by SS guards with machine guns. One lived in hope that one day you would see the outside world again. As long as people around you were going home, there was hope even amidst such daily horror and brutality.

CHAPTER 3

FREEDOM AND EMIGRATION

In May 1939, at the age of seventeen, Willy said farewell to his family at Bonn railway station. He and his cousin Margot Lowy were emigrating to England at the same time and they left together that day. They faced an uncertain future, but with the anticipation that whatever it held for them, at least they should be safe. The whole family turned out at the railway station to see them off; this included Willy's father, mother, brother Manfred, aunts, uncles, and twin sister Thea who was not yet leaving for England. It was, as Willy says, 'a very emotional goodbye. No one knew what lay ahead, although we could all see that it looked terribly grim for those left behind in Germany. The only person I ever saw again was my twin sister Thea [Dorothea].' The train took Willy and Margot from Bonn to Flushing in Holland. It was an immense relief to finally cross the border:

> I was so happy when we crossed the frontier into Holland; only then I felt freedom. I was constantly worried that something might happen before we got there and that we wouldn't get through. It was not uncommon for trains to be held up en route by SS officers and Jewish people turned back. It was a very tense time until we were over that border.

Willy was unable to take much out of Germany. His worldly possessions consisted of a handful of items: a tiny leather suitcase with a few clothes and toiletries, family photographs, a watch which his eldest sister had given him on his bar mitzvah and a fountain pen. He had a wallet with passport, identity card and ten shillings. And that was it. With the ten shillings he bought half a pint of beer during the sea-crossing from Flushing to Harwich and recalls: 'I was so seasick from the crossing and the beer that I couldn't wait to get off.'

Finally England came into view – the country which was to offer Willy sanctuary, albeit then on a temporary visa. From Harwich he and Margot took a train to London's Liverpool Street where his former boss Mr Herz was waiting. They were taken to Mr and Mrs Herz's home at 68 Highfield Avenue in Golders Green, North-West London. The following morning Willy was taken to Bloomsbury House, the centre of Jewish relief from where the Jewish community coordinated work and support for newly arrived refugees from Nazism. One of Willy's memories of that day remains:

> We were early and Bloomsbury House was not yet open, so Mrs Herz took me to a Lyons Teashop. I had my first taste of a proper English breakfast with tea, toast and real marmalade. This all impressed me so much.

Afterwards, he came before the Refugee Committee at Bloomsbury House, who gave him a railway ticket to Bude on the north Cornish coast. His place of work was going to be Wrasford Farm, just outside the seaside town. The following day Willy embarked on the 250-mile train journey to Bude. He was met at the station by the farmer, Mr Hayward. What he had not expected was to be driven back to the farm in a Rolls Royce.

> Mr Hayward was exceptionally kind to me. My English was non-existent, something which we both found difficult. But he was very patient with me. When we arrived at the farm, he introduced me to his son who ran the farm. It was an enormous farm. The food was fantastic. They

made their own butter, had plenty of milk and lots of meat. It was really self-sufficient.

Willy worked at Wrasford Farm for nearly two months during May and June 1939. During his time there he was taught how to ride horses. One of his jobs each day was to round up the cows on horseback with Mr Hayward's son. Whilst he was busy working, Mr Hayward, well aware of the plight of his parents and the possible danger they were in, tried to get permits to bring them and his brother out of Germany. In spite of huge efforts, he was ultimately unsuccessful. Although Willy was surrounded by well-meaning and caring people, he missed his family terribly. He had to adjust rapidly and his knowledge of English was minimal.

The clouds of war were gathering across Europe. In spite of British Prime Minister Neville Chamberlain's efforts to avert war with a number of attempts to appease Hitler, nothing could ultimately turn the tide of events. One of the emergency measures which came into force was the creation of restricted areas around the coast of Britain. Any German refugees living in a restricted zone had to leave immediately, and the coastal region around Bude became one such area.

Willy returned to London and stayed for a few days in a hostel in Cricklewood, North London. He reported back to the Jewish Refugee Committee at Bloomsbury House in central London. His entry visa into Britain required him to be working in agriculture and so he knew that he had to find another post. The Jewish Refugee Committee sent him to a farm inland in Sussex. By now his English had improved, but the experience at this new farm was in stark contrast to his time at Wrasford Farm:

The experience was horrible. It was a much smaller farm and I arrived during the hay-making season. The work was hard but there was nothing wrong with that. I was used to hard labour from my time in Dachau, but it was my overall treatment that was so dreadful. I was paid 2 shillings and 6 pence. All other workers got one pound or two pounds for the same work and same number of hours.

Back in Bonn, efforts were under way to get Willy's twin sister Thea out of Germany. Finally she was granted permission to emigrate to England as a domestic servant. A number of female Jewish refugees successfully entered Britain on domestic permits on condition that they enter the service of a household. In June 1939 Thea left Germany, making her emotional farewells at Bonn railway station. It was the last time she saw her parents and brother Manfred. She wrote to Willy to inform him of the details of her arrival. Willy asked the farmer in Sussex to grant him a couple days leave to meet his sister when she arrived in England. 'He took some persuading,' says Willy, 'because he was often so nasty to me. But he did eventually agree.' Willy had saved his earnings to pay for the train fare. He travelled to London and stayed overnight with a friend in Sussex Gardens off Marble Arch. He was waiting on the platform at Liverpool Street station to greet Thea off the train:

> My cousin Margot came with me to the station, where we waited anx-
> iously but excitedly for Thea. It was a marvellous reunion for us. Thea
> told us about events in Bonn; that the Nazis had forced our parents
> to move to a one-room place in a ghetto area where only Jews were
> allowed to live. But she was very careful to shelter me from the true
> extent of their hardship and suffering. She did not want to make me
> too unhappy.

Whilst conditions had significantly deteriorated for their parents, the Hirschfelds back in Bonn lived in the knowledge that two of their children were safe in Britain. Thea went off to Birmingham to work in the household of a family who had agreed to employ her as a domestic servant. Willy returned to the farm in Sussex, but not for long. He was desperately unhappy:

> The farmer was verbally nasty to me. He was not anti-Jewish but he was
> certainly anti-German. And that affected how he treated me. By now
> we knew war could come at any moment and maybe that accounted
> for some of the farmer's treatment of me – he was just downright anti-
> German. Although I was not one to complain, I was never given enough

food on the farm. My sister supported me at this time. Thea had already been sending me extra money from her wages. That meant I could write to her regularly and afford postage stamps. I had nothing to lose, so I hatched a plan to run away.

Willy devised the escape plan around his early morning shift. Every morning at 5 a.m. he had to bring in five cows to milk. After having milked them, it was his task to take the large urn in a handcart to the main road and put it on a wooden platform. At a certain time it was collected by someone else and taken to the nearest village. One morning Willy took his suitcase and hid it under the wooden platform. The following day he took the milk urn as usual on the handcart and waited for the horse and cart. Eventually he saw it coming towards him. The man agreed to take him to the railway station in the nearest village. Willy made his way back to London, arriving at Victoria station. He had but ten pennies in his pocket. He did not dare ring up his former boss Mr Herz for help because he would not approve of him running away. He proceeded to cross the city and head for Bloomsbury House again. He explained to the Jewish Refugee Committee the terrible conditions under which he had worked on the farm in Sussex. The members were sympathetic and gave him three vouchers, worth a shilling each, to stay the night at Rowton House, a hostel in Whitechapel in the East End. Meals were provided by the nearby soup kitchen. By now war had been declared. That affected the kind of work that Willy carried out. During the day he was employed in the city filling up sandbags to protect banks and financial businesses from possible German bombing.

After a few weeks he took up employment in Whitechapel with a Jewish firm called Rose and Co. The company fitted sewing machines for factories which were manufacturing khaki uniforms for the British army. He comments:

I managed to get my agricultural permit changed to a general working permit. I then found accommodation in Whitechapel High Street above a Jewish tobacconist shop. There were lots of Russian Jews in the area. Everywhere sewing machines were being installed in factories and shops.

Every available space was being utilized to prepare for war. Blackouts were being prepared. The company I worked for fitted benches for sewing machines, which were all powered by one big rod. Our foreman was rather crafty. He refused to install the electric required for the sewing machines unless we were given beer money! And that way we earned extra on top of our earnings.

Willy enjoyed the hustle and bustle of Jewish East End life. It was teaming with Yiddisher culture, something which he had never come across in Bonn. There was so much diversity, particularly amongst the Russian Jews there. Yiddish was spoken in the shops. For the first time he did not feel like a foreigner in a strange land:

I loved the food, especially bean and barley soup with bread, and the salt beef sandwiches. At that time it was possible to get bean and barley soup for about 8d. and a salt beef sandwich for 10d. I didn't need a lot of money at that time to eat well and enjoy myself. Of course everything was closed on a Saturday for the Sabbath. I wasn't alone in not being able to speak English because most of the people around me couldn't speak the language. If you can speak German, it is easy to understand Yiddish. I therefore had no problem in the shops locally. But all my workmates only spoke English and gradually my ability at English improved. I lived in a tiny furnished room over a tobacconist shop. I only had a bed, a wardrobe, and a chair but I was happy. The toilet and washbasin were on another floor, so once a week I went to the local public baths to have a shower. At weekends I went to a church hall in Kingsbury in North London where we helped in a hostel for young Jewish refugee children. We played games with them. There was a group of us who helped out. It was always a long way back to the East End. I went to the cinema a lot. I always went to the exciting market in Petticoat Lane on Sundays.

Just before war broke out, Willy went to his first ever football league match at Arsenal stadium in Highbury, North London. He had become friendly with a sergeant at the local police station in the East End and it was he who introduced him as an Arsenal supporter. He got tickets for both of them to see a match at Highbury. As Willy comments, 'this was the beginning of a long love affair with Arsenal.'

At this time Willy was still able to write to his parents in Bonn. Occasionally he received letters back from them, but they were not able to write about their living conditions in Germany.

> They were too afraid to put anything in writing. They couldn't tell me how bad it had got. If they had, the letters would never have left Germany but would have been censored. Unfortunately their letters were destroyed when some of my belongings, which were in storage, were lost in the bombings of the East End in the war. For a short time after the beginning of the war, Thea was able to write to our parents through the Red Cross, but eventually all communication stopped and we worried for their safety.

At 11 a.m. on 3 September 1939 Britain declared war on Germany after German troops crossed the border into Poland. Prime Minister Chamberlain broadcast to the nation a radio speech which Willy heard:

> I am speaking to you from No. 10 Downing Street. This morning the British Ambassador in Berlin handed the German government a final note, stating that unless the British government heard from them by eleven o'clock that they were prepared at once to withdraw their troops from Poland, a state of war would exist between us. I have to tell you now that no such undertaking has been received and that consequently this country is at war with Germany.

'It was no great surprise,' says Willy, 'that Britain was at war with my former country. It had been coming for a long time. I had lived through all that was going on in Germany and could see no way back. Hitler had grandiose ideas of power; he had singled out Jews initially as the targets of his racial hatred and blamed us for Germany's misfortunes. Not for nothing had he amassed a huge army.'

Within minutes of Chamberlain's announcement, the air-raid sirens sounded. The country was plunged into an uncertain future. With the outbreak of war, Willy found himself in an unusual position. He did not have British nationality and was still technically a German. Along with thousands of other German and Austrian émigrés living in Britain, his status changed overnight and he became classed as an 'enemy alien'. In the coming year, this was to have a number of consequences for him. One was that every enemy alien had to appear before a tribunal to assess their security risk to Britain. Each had to be placed in one of three categories: A, B or C; A being those most at risk to national security, i.e. Nazi sympathisers. In the autumn of 1939 Willy appeared before the local tribunal: 'They asked me a number of questions. Why I was here, what I was doing. Once they knew I had been in a concentration camp, they knew I was a genuine case.' As a refugee from Nazi oppression he was placed in category C and exempt from internment. This meant that he could carry on working in the East End with no restrictions.

Meanwhile, on 15 November, Willy's sister Thea was summoned to appear before a tribunal in Warwick. Her tribunal papers note her residence as Earlswood Road, Dorridge, near Birmingham, and her place of employment as Orchard Close. Like her brother, she was also 'exempt from internment and special restrictions'. The statement signed by the presiding person further said: 'I am satisfied that this alien is ready to help this country and is unlikely to do anything harmful to the national interest.'

But Thea was not happy in her post in Birmingham. Willy secured a new job for her in London working as a housemaid to his boss, Mr Rose, and nanny to his young daughter. By Christmas 1939, Thea was happily settled in Finchley, North-West London. Willy recalls the generosity of their boss: 'On Boxing Day that year Mr Rose gave each of us £5 to go out and enjoy ourselves. It was a lot of money then.'

Life was about to change for Willy. On 9 April 1940 Nazi forces moved into Denmark and occupied the country, although Hitler permitted Danish self-government as a Protectorate until 1943. Events were rapidly changing. A month later, on 10 May, the German military machine swept into Holland, Belgium, Luxembourg and France. The speed of the advance was alarming. Britain looked to be next. The British government ordered the immediate evacuation of nearly 300,000 British troops from the beaches of Dunkirk in an epic rescue operation using every available vessel. It was successful, but panic gripped the nation. All efforts were focused on securing areas where German forces might attempt an invasion. That meant evacuating any German or Austrian refugees living in such areas, usually on or near the coast. The eyes of government turned to German, Austrian and Italian refugees living in Britain, the 'enemy aliens'. They could be infiltrated by German spies and no one would be able to ascertain who was loyal to Britain as a genuine refugee or who was a 'Fifth Columnist' (spy). It was one of the first issues that new prime minister Winston Churchill had to face when he took over the reins of government on 10 May 1940. His advisers suggested the only practical solution open to him was the mass internment of enemy aliens. He implemented this policy as a matter of urgency, coining the phrase 'collar the lot'. In a speech, Churchill said:

> We have found it necessary to take measures of increasing stringency, not only against enemy aliens and suspicious characters of other nationalities, but also against British subjects who may become a danger or a nuisance should the war be transported to the United Kingdom. I know there are a great number of people affected by the orders which we have made who are passionate enemies of Nazi Germany. I am sorry for them, but we cannot at the present time and under the present stress, draw all the distinctions which we should like to do.

Nearly 30,000 Germans, Austrians and Italians received an early morning visit from the local policeman who had come to arrest them. Many had been working in academic institutions and businesses since 1933, but they were still taken from their homes into custody. Once they were interned, the rationale for this policy was hotly disputed. They remained behind barbed wire for several months, sometimes longer, while Parliament debated their situation. The majority were interned on the Isle of Man, living in requisitioned hotels and boarding houses. Other internees were sent to makeshift internment camps across mainland Britain, Canada and also Australia. The numerous camps on the Isle of Man became a microcosm of central European intellect with the formation of a mini university, an orchestra and the Amadeus Quartet. Among them were some of Europe's finest intellectuals: artists, sculptors, scientists, musicians, doctors, surgeons and professors.

Britain was facing its darkest hour. The Norwegian campaign had failed, leading to the resignation of Prime Minister Chamberlain. Belgium had surrendered and British troops had endured a humiliating evacuation from the beaches around Dunkirk. In taking over government, Winston Churchill boosted the resolve and morale of the nation in a rallying speech in the Commons on 4 June. His words that day have become immortalised as amongst his finest:

> We shall fight on the beaches, we shall fight on the landing grounds, we shall fight in the fields and in the streets, we shall fight in the hills; we shall never surrender.

For Willy, who had seen the might of the Nazi war machine, these words were a much-needed boost:

> We feared like everyone else that Britain really would be next. Invasion was a real possibility at that time. And that sent shockwaves through me because, after all, I had seen so much terror and brutality in Germany. Churchill's words were the backbone of strength which rallied the British people at one of the most difficult periods of the war. For me, at that time, being a German refugee with a strong German accent living in Britain could be fraught with dangers, especially if people did not understand that I was a refugee. I usually had chance to explain and then I was always welcome. But there was, understandably, a lot of anti-German feeling around. Memories of the First World War with Germany just twenty-one years earlier were still very vivid in people's minds. After all, my father had fought for Germany against the British then, but now I depended on Britain's protection.

In spite of being classified 'C' (a friendly alien) by the Aliens Tribunal, Willy was not immune from the internment policy. After a year living in the safety of Britain he found himself arrested. It was a familiar but worrying scenario: first arrested by the Nazis landing him in Dachau, and now internment behind barbed wire by British authorities. It was a time full of uncertainties about the future. His only consolation was that he was not alone. He was to undergo the same experience as nearly 30,000 other enemy aliens; but not that of his sister Thea, who was not interned. Willy recalls:

> One early morning in June 1940, I was visited by a policeman at my lodgings and he asked me to go with him to Lemon Street police station. It was only then that I was told that I would be interned. I was allowed to take a few basic things with me. The police officer wasn't allowed to tell me any more details. My boss Mr Ross discovered that I was at the local police station and came to try and get me out. He argued tooth and nail that I was needed for essential war work. It fell on deaf ears. Mr Ross then proceeded to offer £50 for my release, a huge sum of money in those days. He was refused. I was no threat to national security but of course that didn't matter. There was no time to assess who was who. We suffered from a blanket policy to 'collar the lot', as Churchill said.

Willy was driven by van to Kempton Park Racecourse in Surrey. There he joined several hundred other male internees camped under canvas on the racecourse. He remained there for a couple of weeks. The internees were well looked after and received decent food. Willy made new friends and spent most of the time playing cards. From Kempton Park he was transferred by train, with other internees, to Huyton near Liverpool, a requisitioned housing estate surrounded by barbed wire. By the time he arrived, there were already around 2,000 internees there. Willy explains:

> There were not enough houses for all of us, so some were allocated tents. Nothing much happened in Huyton. We had our own entertainment because amongst the internees was Rawicz and Landauer, who were later very famous after the war. They played the piano. I had already made a lot of friends. There was a group of about six of us including myself who stuck together right through the war: Gerry Moore (Gerhard Moses), Joe Milton (Joseph Minz), Franz, Kurt Mongenroth and Herbert.

For me, I was not unduly bothered by the turn of events. I was young and it was just another adventure to me. For the older ones, it was a different matter – some never really adjusted to internment.

Willy and his new group of friends were in Huyton for about a week. Then news came that they were about to be moved. It was rumoured that Canada was their destination. The government had already shipped one load of internees there and another troopship was assigned to transport 1,500 more at the beginning of July.

The SS *Arandora Star* set sail on 1 July 1940; its destination: Canada. On the second day, disaster struck when the ship was torpedoed by a German U-boat off the coast of Ireland, resulting in great loss of life. Out of the 1,500 internees aboard, it was estimated that over 700 died from drowning. Survivors were pulled from the freezing waters and taken back to internment camps, only to be hoarded onto another troopship just days later with Willy and his friends.

On 3 July, in spite of the tragedy of the *Arandora Star*, another troopship left Liverpool: HMT *Ettrick*, bound for Canada. On 4 July a Polish liner, SS *Sobieski*, carrying 1,000 refugees and 500 German POWs, left Glasgow, also for Canada. Both ships arrived safely at their destinations. A week after they had set sail, Willy was among internees transferred from Huyton to Liverpool docks. The atmosphere was tense:

I can never forget the scene that greeted our arrival. A large grey troopship was docked at the quayside. It loomed above us. Then we knew that we were about to be transported, but we had no idea where. We thought it was to be Canada. Crossing the Atlantic with the constant threat of U-boats was no joke but we had no choice. We were about to depart for an unknown destination.

That ship was a three-year-old grey liner called the *Dunera* which had been converted into a troopship. Bewildered internees walked up the gangway to an uncertain future. As the line of people slowly moved forward onto the ship, they were ruthlessly and roughly searched by British soldiers with fixed bayonets. Documents and passports were torn up, valuables taken and suitcases confiscated. Having only been in Britain for a year or two, they had very few possessions anyway. Now what little they had was taken away. 'It was a demoralising and degrading experience,' recalls Willy. 'We were searched and everyone had their things taken. I didn't have a suitcase, only a carrier bag of essentials, so I was fortunate not really to lose anything much.'

Having been manhandled, sometimes quite brutally, the internees were pushed towards the bowels of the ship. All this had occurred under the watchful gaze of Lieutenant-Colonel Scott and First Lieutenant O'Neill, who had done nothing to intervene. They were the masters of the ship, but did not step in to prevent the injustices they were witnessing. The internees were about to embark on what would be a nightmare journey.

CHAPTER 4

HM TROOPSHIP *DUNERA*

At 2 a.m. on 11 July 1940, HM troopship *Dunera* set sail from Liverpool on a journey which, unknown to the internees, would take nine weeks and would land them in Australia. Aboard were 2,000 refugees from Nazi oppression, the majority Jews but also among them non-Jewish artists, musicians and communists. They did not know where they were heading. The authorities made sure their destination was a closely guarded secret.

Much to the refugees' dismay, the ship was also carrying 251 German and 200 Italian prisoners of war, all 'Category A' prisoners deemed a threat to national security. The British soldiers guarding the internees did not distinguish between genuine refugees and Nazi POWs. The 12,600-tonne *Dunera*, built in 1937 and converted from a passenger vessel to a troopship, was totally unsuited to the transportation of so many men. Her maximum capacity was just 1,600 people including the crew. When she sailed in the early hours of 11 July, she was dangerously overcrowded with 2,000 internees on board, 1,000 men over its capacity. Conditions were appalling, likened by many to those of a floating concentration camp. Willy recalls:

All the gangways were barbed wired so no one could escape. People were pushed around, some beaten up. We were treated like German prisoners, not refugees from Nazi oppression. We were immediately taken below deck where there were no port holes for fresh air. Neither daylight nor fresh air ever reached below deck for the whole of our journey. Ventilation was poor. We were in very cramped conditions with little room to walk about. There were only large wooden tables and benches, and several hammocks in various corners which were occupied by the older internees. Blankets were issued to us and we had to make do with that. It was all very primitive and uncomfortable. And of course our conditions did not improve one iota during the nine weeks we were aboard. My friends and I stayed together. We arranged our sleeping as best we could, some of us on top of the table and some underneath on the iron deck. The lights were always dim, during the day and night. One internee was so traumatised by the whole experience that, in spite of security, he managed to throw himself overboard and drowned.

On 12 July, less than forty-eight hours after leaving the port of Liverpool, the *Dunera* took a direct hit from German submarine *U-56* off the coast of Ireland. Willy remembers it:

On the second or third night of our journey we experienced a very loud crash. Confined below deck, we had no idea what it was, although we suspected it to be a torpedo. The ship rocked. All hell broke out. People panicked and tried to get to the exits but these were locked. We were later told that we had been the target of a German submarine. The torpedo had failed to go off and we were saved. There would have been no chance of us ever getting out of the ship had disaster struck.

On high sea a lot of the internees' luggage and papers were thrown overboard. The U-boat surfaced the following day and found German documents floating in the sea. The commanding officer believed that the *Dunera* was carrying only German POWs and therefore did not attempt to torpedo the ship again. The *Dunera* continued the rest of the journey safely, but it was still to be a harrowing nine-week ordeal in appalling conditions amidst much personal mistreatment by the British soldiers. The lack of any personal possessions was not the only humiliation suffered by the internees. They were confined below deck for twenty-three hours a day with a maximum of only one hour's exercise above deck. When they did receive some exercise, they were often pushed around by the guards and suffered verbal abuse. The upper part of the ship was out of bounds, the access barred by barbed wire and soldiers with bayonets. As Willy confirmed, below deck the internees slept in three layers with one group sleeping on the deck, another on long tables and benches, and the third on hammocks strung above the tables. Most suffered terrible seasickness. The sanitary arrangements were spartan with only ten toilets for 2,000 men. They had no change of clothing and inadequate washing facilities. One internee, whom Willy remembers, was Anton Walter Freud, a grandson of Sigmund Freud. Walter Freud wrote about his time on the *Dunera* in his unpublished memoirs *Before the Anticlimax*, quoted in the author's previously published work *Freuds' War*. Freud's mathematical brain calculated that if all ten toilets were in use all the time, then each internee would have just seven minutes a day for their requirements. Willy concurs with Freud's memory of the sanitary arrangements:

> The toilet facilities were totally inadequate. They were open cubicles without doors; there was also a shower room which we used. The toilets were overflowing, the buckets were full and the air below deck smelt of urine. There was always someone standing outside the toilet, handing out toilet paper. We were only allowed two pieces. We were allowed occasionally on deck to exercise and get fresh air. Even then we were always guarded by the soldiers. Most internees were seasick which meant that with the lack of ventilation aboard ship, the smell was often unbearable and the mess terrible.

A detailed nine-page report of the horrendous conditions on the *Dunera* and mistreatment of internees was eventually compiled by a camp spokesman in Australia and sent to the British High Commissioner in Canberra. It was dated 2 December 1940 and spares no details of their treatment. It covers issues of how the internees were selected to be sent to Australia, most agreeing to go voluntarily having had assurances of a better life. It reports that those who came from Camp Lingfield, about 350 men, were not given any information and were therefore totally unprepared for the long journey. Willy, who came from Kempton Park Racecourse, says that was also true for their internees. The report reads that the *Dunera* was overcrowded by at least fifty per cent and that 'in the event of an accident the congestion alone would have made an attempt at life saving impossible'. Willy recalls the potentially dangerous conditions:

> Buckets for urine were provided. The buckets were soon overflowing and sewerage flooded the decks as the ship rolled. In the midst of it men were lying on the floor to sleep, for at first there were neither hammocks nor blankets. For weeks the hatches were kept battened down. Neither daylight nor natural air ever reached the decks. For weeks one was dependent on electric light and artificial air supply through ventilation and that on overcrowded decks through the tropics. No inoculation against typhoid and cholera was administered in spite of circumstances obviously favouring an epidemic of this kind. Although the most essential medicaments were lacking, vital medicines like insulin were thrown overboard when discovered to be owned by the internees.

It was always much harder for the older internees who had been used to a relatively comfortable life. The young ones tended to adjust more easily to the conditions. Meals were basic but adequate:

> We were organised by tables for our meals. Every table had a leader, and two men from each table had to collect the food from the galley. I was lucky and never seasick. I had more food because those who were seasick couldn't eat much. The food was edible and bearable. Franz, my friend, was a pastry cook by trade. He was lucky during the journey to work at the officer's mess baking and helping in the kitchen. Occasionally he smuggled a few rolls out to give us.

The monotony of the long hours below deck was relieved with numerous activities which the internees arranged among themselves. As in the internment camps on the Isle of Man, the *Dunera* had among its 'passengers' a number of intellectuals: doctors, scientists, musicians and professors. Lectures were arranged and games of cards played. Willy recalls that one internee made a set of chess figures from dough. Some organised chess tournaments while others entertained by telling stories or singing songs. During the journey, artist Robert Hofmann made a pencil portrait of Willy, the original of which he still has to this day. It is signed and dated 4 August 1940.

The *Dunera* docked four times en route to Australia: at Freetown in Sierra Leone, Takoradi (Gold Coast, now Ghana), Cape Town in South Africa and Fremantle in Western Australia. Between North Africa and landing in Australia, fresh water was only supplied two or three times a week. Conditions and treatment were still so bad that the elder internees who had survived Nazi brutality in the concentration camps now feared for their lives at the hands of the British guards. They often tried to hide whenever they saw a man in uniform coming, especially when the ship docked at a port where the guards often got drunk and their behaviour worsened. The psychological scars of these internees ran deep.

The *Dunera* docked at Freetown on the morning of 24 July, and then on to Takoradi, arriving there on 27 July. Willy comments:

We still did not know where we were going, but we had on the ship some intellectuals. One of them was an astronomer. He looked at the stars when on deck. He told us: 'I think we are on our way to Africa!' He was right. Then I found a small porthole which we could open slightly. We took it in turns to stand there to take fresh air. Sometimes we saw flying fish. By now we were close to the African coast. We were told it was Takoradi. We were so near that we could even see African soldiers guarding the coast.

The ship remained in dock in Takoradi for two days. On 29 July it left for Cape Town:

Our next stop was Cape Town. I volunteered to help load food onto the ship. About seven of us were allowed to do this. Our job was to carry cases of apples onto the *Dunera*. They were in very flimsy boxes. I dropped one on purpose and we all filled our pockets with apples. This was special. I gave all my friends an apple when I got back below deck. They called it 'manna from heaven', and something they have never forgotten. We were lucky to get away with it because the guards guarding us were

South Africans. It became clear after South Africa that we were heading for Australia or New Zealand. My friends and I had talked already what we would do in Australia. We planned that on arrival we would report to the kitchen for duties. We also decided that we would organise football and sport. We wouldn't sit around and do nothing. Going through the tropics was the worst time, if there could be such a thing. We had no adequate washing facilities, no toothbrushes or toothpaste and no hair-brushes or combs. We were sticky and sweaty, with no proper means for basic hygiene. It was simply terrible.

The *Dunera* had arrived at Cape Town on 8 August, leaving again the following day. The next port of call was Fremantle, Australia, arriving on 27 August. After twenty-four hours there, it left for Melbourne and arrived on 3 September. At Melbourne, the German and Italian POWs were disembarked. The following day at 7 a.m. the ship departed with the remaining internees for the last part of its journey. By this time the men had grown unkempt beards, not having been able to shave aboard ship because all razors had been confiscated. To save any embarrassment with the Australian authorities, the internees were issued with a couple of razors to share in order to make themselves tidy for disembarkation. During their nine-week journey, they were oblivious that they had left behind a Britain fighting for survival. In the skies over southern England the Battle of Britain pilots were struggling in dog-fights with the German Luftwaffe. The outcome was uncertain. Britain's future hung in the balance. None of this ever reached the ears of the '*Dunera* boys'. They were unaware of what was happening in the war, not knowing whether Britain had been overrun by German forces.

At 11 a.m. on 6 September 1940 the *Dunera* finally reached Sydney harbour after nine weeks at sea in horrific conditions. The internees disembarked and were directed straight onto trains. Willy recalls:

It was a relief to have finally arrived in Sydney harbour, although we did not see much of it then because we were taken straight off the boat. Thereafter Australian guards took over. They behaved fantastically towards us and were very friendly and kind. But at the dockside we noticed a lot of people watching us disembark. Apparently they were expecting German prisoners of war and were surprised to see young and elderly men in civilian clothing. But that didn't stop them shouting abuse at us. I didn't know what they were saying because my English wasn't good enough, but their tone was angry and jeering. We walked to the railway station under guard and then boarded a very long train. It had windows and proper seats. We didn't know where we were going. For the first time we saw civilians, including women. They behaved fantastically towards us and were very friendly and kind. On the train we were given sandwiches, drinks and fresh fruit.

Unknown to the refugees, they faced a nineteen-hour train journey across Australia to Hay in New South Wales. Their new destination was located 750km from Sydney in a very dry, hot and barren region of Australia, several miles from the nearest settlement. They were being accommodated in two adjacent camps named Hay 7 and Hay 8, not far from the Murrumbidgee River. Willy's fellow internee Father Koenig, a German Jesuit priest, later wrote: 'It wasn't the luxury camp we had been told about during the trip through the Indian Ocean … we found ourselves completely isolated, on the edge of a boundless, almost treeless, plain.' The climate was hot, humid and totally unsuitable for the internees who found it hard to adjust. They were divided into two groups, approximately 800 men to each camp. Willy and his friends found themselves in camp Hay 8. Each camp was surrounded by barbed wire and watchtowers, guarded by Australian soldiers:

It consisted of lines of wooden huts with approximately thirty internees per hut. We slept in rows of bunks. These were comfortable with mattresses and blankets. Within a few days everything was organised. As planned, my friends and I headed for the kitchen. There were a few more internees who did the same thing. The camp had two kitchens and two dining rooms, each serving 400 people. We were lucky that one of our internees was an Austrian chef who took charge of the kitchen. The guards knew we were coming, but they were expecting Italian POWs, not Germans and Austrians. In the first few days after our arrival, we only got Italian food! The store food had plenty of ravioli and spaghetti which we cooked until everyone was fed up with it! Eventually everything changed and we received Australian food. We were never short of food or water. There were no war rations in Australia and we had plenty of meat, often lamb. My first job in the kitchen was to help early in the morning with the breakfast, making porridge for 400 internees. My other friends were given different work. Franz and Gerry were ordered to be the bakers. Their work was done at night, baking bread and rolls for the next day. We had all the freedom we wanted from the camp commander to make life easy.

The kitchen was well organised with a store, cooks, bakers, potato peelers, plate washers, wood choppers and stokers. Everything was worked out in two shifts. A cleaning party was formed for hygiene shifts to clean toilets, showers, wash houses, boilers and dust bins. A camp leader was elected by the internees, one for every hut. As with internment camps back in England, the intellectuals at Hay formed a camp university. Lectures were given by professors and academics who were leading specialists in their subjects. These included history, art, literature and economics. Mathematical problems were sometimes worked out on the labels of empty jam jars. Languages were also popular: French, Russian, Italian, Latin, Greek, Czech and Portuguese. Concerts and shows were organised by the musicians and actors. Among them was musician Ray Martin who formed a band called 'Hay Days'. Renowned pianist Peter Stadlen was also there. The internees composed their own camp song:

Say Hay for Happy,
and you feel snappy,
and you don't want to die.
Even if you sell your overcoat,
for just the sight
of one more bite
of tasty butterbrot.

A bank opened with its own specially printed money which was not legal tender outside the camp. One shilling, two shillings and sixpence notes were printed. Willy remembers:

It was great because it enabled us to buy things from the canteen. I was paid in camp money for working in the kitchen and was able to buy cigarettes from the canteen. I often bought tobacco because it was cheaper to roll my own. Two Austrian internees ran a coffee bar and we were able to pay for coffee and cakes with camp money. Much of our time was spent playing cards. We had bridge tournaments.

The talent in the camp was extraordinary. Much ingenuity was employed to make the best of life. No items were wasted or thrown away that could be recycled as something else. With Willy working in the kitchen he saved what he could:

When our supply of food came in, it was in bags of cotton material. There was no plastic packaging then. I kept the empty bags which had had sugar, flour, etc in and gave them to my friend Mr Heyman who was a qualified tailor. He washed them and eventually made shorts for us. One guy made hot water bottles, but I can't now remember what he made them from. There was so much talent in that camp that it made for an interesting time.

Football became a very important focus for Willy and his friends. The grounds of the camp were large enough for a full-size football pitch. Willy was in his element:

We were fortunate to have an Austrian who had been in charge of the Austrian football league. He immediately organised a football league and teams. My friends and I started playing football and arranged our own team with Franz as captain. Gerry and I called the team 'Amateure'. It didn't take us long to set up the pitch with two goal posts. A Jewish organisation in Sydney sent us footballs and boots. There was no grass in this part of Australia so we played football on the dusty earth, but that didn't matter. We loved it and were never bored.

By now back in England, male internees on the Isle of Man and camps around the country were being enlisted in the 'alien' Pioneer Corps, a non-combatant unit of the British army. The government realised that the internees in Australia could also be recruited for the British army, so in March 1941 Major Julian Layton was sent out to Hay with the express purpose of enlisting internees into the Pioneer Corps. Major Layton was accustomed to working with refugees from Nazi oppression, having had dealings with them in Kitchener Camp, a refugee-transit camp near Sandwich in Kent. When Major Layton arrived at Hay in Australia, the internees were given opportunity to talk about the possibilities in the army. Willy recalls:

> My friends and I, that included Gerry, Joe, Kurt and Franz, decided that we wanted to go back to England and join the Pioneer Corps. We were vetted, only category C internees (most of us) could join the army. We had to be between the age of eighteen and fifty. We could have stayed in Australia because as an alternative I knew we would eventually be released for an Australian Labour Corps. We didn't. We wanted to return to England. Major Layton couldn't tell us when we would return because he was waiting for a ship to take us back. Approximately 400–500 decided to enlist in the Pioneer Corps. Some groups left earlier than us, like Walter Freud who returned on SS *Gleniffer*.

One of the first decisions Major Layton made on arriving at the two camps was to declare them unsuitable for those who had enlisted in the army. The humid climate and sand storms made conditions very difficult. Willy recalls one incident when he and his friends had prepared afternoon tea of Welsh rarebit for over 400 people. This was simple to make with bread, butter and cheese which was then baked, but just before it was served up, a tremendous sandstorm blew up. All 400 Welsh rarebits were covered in a layer of sand and rendered inedible. They had to be thrown away and something else hurriedly prepared. Three hundred and forty internees who had enlisted for the Pioneer Corps were soon moved to an alternative camp. They were transferred by train from Hay to Tatura in Victoria. It was a twelve-hour journey that would take them across New South Wales:

It was a comfortable and pleasant journey. My friends and I managed to sit together in the same compartment. We always did everything together. The train was guarded. We crossed the Murray River where the landscape changed dramatically and was much greener.

The climate at Tatura was more suitable than Hay. The camp was surrounded by lush green countryside and orchards. The nearest town was Shepperton, but the internees remained in camp. Accommodation consisted of small huts, two men in each. 'There was a wooden bunk bed in each hut,' says Willy, 'but as soon as we got our allocated hut, we found a saw and sawed them in half to make it more comfortable.' Willy again took charge in the kitchen, with the help of his friends. He cooked for around 300 internees each day.

We had wonderful rations. The camp commander and I sat down once a week to decide the menu for the next seven days. By now I had had enough experience of cooking from our time in Hay. There were not many activities for us in Tatura, so life could be quite boring at times. We kept busy with activities in the kitchen, preparing food during the day and in the evenings chatted in a circle.

After a while they were moved from Tatura to another camp, Bamara in Southern Australia. This time they faced a twenty-eight-hour train journey across Australia. 'We saw a lot of Australia,' muses Willy, 'all courtesy of the government.' Looking out the window, it was not an infrequent sight to see kangaroos hopping along beside the train. The camp at Bamara was similar in size to Hay. The men were housed in huts, with around twenty per hut. Again, Willy and his friends worked in the kitchens. It was here that he celebrated his twenty-first birthday on 17 August 1941.

It turned out to be a really memorable birthday. My friend Franz was the camp cook. He made wine which was forbidden! We got quite drunk, but we had a wonderful party. The camp commander who was a high-ranking Australian officer surprised me with a fruit basket. It was an amazing day.

Just before returning to England, there was one final journey to be made across Australia, this time by train to Melbourne which took a total of twenty-two hours; then from Melbourne to a small camp at Liverpool just outside Sydney, a distance which took twenty-four hours by train. There they were well treated again and knew that their journey back to England was imminent.

Eventually, the whole *Dunera* episode was acknowledged by Churchill as 'a deplorable mistake'. The officers and other ranks involved in the mistreatment of the internees on the *Dunera* were court-martialled and severely reprimanded. Until the writing of this book, Willy has always been reluctant to speak about just how bad conditions were.

> After the war, I was quite happy to speak about our time in Australia but not the *Dunera*. I was ashamed of how the British troops treated us because I served in the British forces during the war and nothing could take away my pride in that. But it meant that it was a painful memory to recall how we were treated by soldiers in British army uniform on the *Dunera*.

Willy is philosophical about their time in Australia:

> We felt totally safe in Australia. We knew that Hitler would never invade Australia. Britain was a different matter – invasion was a real possibility in the summer of 1940. If we had remained in internment camps in Britain, and Hitler had invaded its shores, we would have been the first to be sent back to Germany and concentration camps. And that would have been the end of us. Far away, across the other side of the world, we were safe. But I was never more pleased than to return to Britain in the autumn of 1941 to join the British army.

CHAPTER 5

HIS MAJESTY'S FORCES

In the autumn of 1941, the twenty-one-year-old Willy was one of approximately 330 internees who returned to Britain from Australia aboard the SS *Stirling Castle*. That included his five friends Gerry, Joe, Franz, Kurt and Herbert with whom he had spent the past year in Australia. They had no decent clothes or possessions after their internment, so before leaving Australia they were given new clothes from a leading Sydney store, 'David Jones'. On 12 October 1941 the SS *Stirling Castle* left Sydney harbour for the return journey to England.

> When we sailed out of Sydney harbour, passing under the famous Sydney bridge, I remember feeling triumphant. As a soldier in the British army saying goodbye to Australia from the SS *Stirling Castle* was wonderful.

The *Stirling Castle* arrived at the port of Liverpool on 29 November. All the men had agreed to enlist in the British army. The contrast with the outward journey on the *Dunera* could not have been starker:

> We were already treated like British soldiers even though we were still in civilian clothes. We slept in bunk beds with blankets, rather than

hammocks or the hard deck as we had on the *Dunera*. We were very well treated throughout the journey back. We were allowed on deck any time during the day. During the night there was a rigorously enforced black-out – we were in the middle of a war. First we landed in Auckland, New Zealand to pick up air force officers. Our journey then took us through the Panama Canal and most of us stayed up during the night to experience going through the canal. It was actually an exciting journey. While we were waiting on one side of the canal (from the Pacific to the Atlantic), we had to wait a few days before proceeding because the rumour went that there were German U-boats operating in the vicinity. There was always a chance that we might be hit by a U-boat. We had great amusement at this time because a few of the ship's crew caught a shark using a proper line. It took quite a while to hoist it onto the deck.

Amongst the newly released internees aboard the SS *Stirling Castle* were a number of musicians and actors who provided entertainment. They formed a band under the direction of musician Ray Martin and called it 'The Stirling Crazy Gang'. Performances were organised for the other passengers. A rare copy of a programme from that time reveals that on 11 November 1941, at 2.30 p.m. and 8.15 p.m., they presented *We're in Love!!!* which was described as 'a rumbling riot of rollicking revue'. The entertainment featured 'The Stirling Singers' conducted by Kurt Behrens. Amongst their talent were other newly released internees, including Max Lewinsky, Ernest Gumperz, Ray Martin and Rudy Karrell. Rudy became good friends with Willy after the war. They still meet up regularly for coffee. Ray Martin, composer and singer originally from Vienna, composed the music for these performances with Eddie Kassner. He also wrote the script with Peter Land, Alan Ford and Michael Mellinger. After serving in the Pioneer Corps and army intelligence, Ray Martin went on to become a famous musician after the war, recording almost exclusively for Columbia Records and collaborating with Lou Praeger.

While still on the SS *Stirling Castle*, and before docking at Liverpool, the men were officially sworn into the army. As ex-German refugees from Nazi oppression they were required to sign an oath of allegiance to King George VI and his heirs. It was a momentous time for them. Willy comments:

> In the eyes of British law, I was still theoretically a German national because I had originally arrived in England on a German passport. That was the reason why I had to swear loyalty to the British king, even though we did not regard ourselves as German any more. As soon as I came to England, even though I had a German passport, I saw myself as a refugee from Nazi oppression.

Signing the Oath of Allegiance was one step further towards the creation of Willy's new identity. He received the King's Shilling, as did all the enemy aliens and soldiers joining the army. His childhood in Germany now seemed an aeon away. He was then given a railway ticket to whichever destination he chose for a week's leave before army training began.

An unexpected surprise greeted Willy as he arrived at the port of Liverpool. At the dockside his twin sister Thea was waiting for him. She had an inkling that he might be on the ship returning from Australia and had come to the dock to find him. While Willy had been in Australia she had enlisted in the ATS (Auxiliary Territorial Service) along with about a thousand other ex-German and ex-Austrian Jewish refugee women. After initial training she was posted to an army transit camp at Huyton, outside Liverpool. There her duties were limited to cooking and serving in the officers' mess. Rumours circulated that a ship was about to arrive in Liverpool carrying internees from Australia. There was every chance that her brother Willy might be on it. She waited anxiously as the passengers walked down the gangway. She was not disappointed. There was Willy with the five friends whom he had kept close to throughout internment. He recalls:

> It was a huge unexpected surprise for me to see Thea at the dockside. I could not possibly have imagined that she would be waiting for me. It was a very emotional reunion for us. I bought her a gift from Australia – a tin of peaches. Peaches were rare in Britain in wartime. No one ever saw such luxuries, but in Australia it had been easy to get hold of for her.

She was so delighted and it was one of my lasting memories of that day. What a home greeting for me to be reunited with Thea. By now I was already beginning to see Britain as my home.

Willy travelled to London to spend a week's leave with Mr Herz, his former boss from Germany who by now had changed his name to Mr Hearst. He then took the train to the Victorian seaside town of Ilfracombe on the rugged North Devon coast. There he was among the last batch of enemy aliens to be recruited into the non-combatant 'alien' Pioneer Corps. It was the only unit open to him at that time as a non-British citizen, originally of German nationality. None of the new recruits had British nationality. He enlisted as Willy Hirschfeld on 29 November 1941 and was given army number 13807111; the first four digits denoted his status as an enemy alien in the eyes of the British authorities. His five close friends from Australia: Gerry, Joe, Franz, Kurt and Herbert had also enlisted into the army and were trained in the Pioneer Corps with him. Their time in Ilfracombe lasted about six weeks and consisted of square-bashing, marching along the seafront and lectures on army protocol. Willy explains: 'Our training was not hard, just marching and keeping fit. We had no rifles at that time. We were an unarmed labour corps.'

One of the first people Willy met when he arrived was ex-German refugee Harry Rossney (original name Helmuth Rosettenstein), who was assigned to the quartermaster stores in Ilfracombe's Wilder Road to issue all the army uniforms. Willy duly received his kit from Harry, and although their paths only crossed briefly then, they would later become lifelong friends when they met again after the war.

What none of the new recruits from Australia knew until much later was that they were the last of around 6,500 enemy aliens to enlist in the Pioneer Corps. Around 4,000 had already trained during 1940–41 and formed into 'alien' Pioneer companies. The first recruits had enlisted as early as December 1939 in the transit refugee camp called Kitchener Camp near Sandwich in Kent. Of the six companies that were raised there in the spring of 1940, five were sent to France with the British Expeditionary Force (BEF). These were subsequently evacuated from the Dunkirk area in June 1940 after Nazi forces swept into Belgium, Holland and France, routing the BEF. Some of the men with whom Willy was about to serve in various Pioneer companies had enlisted directly from the Isle of Man. They had been released from internment over the summer of 1940 after Parliament had fiercely debated the wisdom of placing any enemy aliens behind barbed wire. At this time, Willy had only just arrived in Australia and was not to be released for another fourteen months. Pioneer companies were sent all over the country performing manual labour tasks: building Britain's coastal defences against invasion, constructing army camps and Nissen huts, carrying out forestry work, or clearing bomb damage in the heavily blitzed areas of London, Bristol and Plymouth.

The contribution of these men to the war is all the more extraordinary and meaningful because without yet being British citizens, they could not be conscripted by the British government. All had to volunteer. Having survived Nazi Germany and Austria, with some like Willy having been in concentration camps, they did not think about self-preservation. They unreservedly volunteered for the British army, although the opportunity to fight in combatant regiments would be denied them for nearly three years. Their full history is told in two other books by the author: *Jews in North Devon during the Second World War* and *The King's Most Loyal Enemy Aliens*. Of army training, Willy recalls:

> We always had a good time in Ilfracombe and we didn't want to leave. It was a town relatively sheltered from the realities of war. Its picturesque harbour was idyllic with its fishing boats. Occasionally we visited the Garrison Theatre which put on shows by our refugees who had musical talent or were actors. One of the shows I saw there was *Babes in the Wood* which featured our commanding officer's daughter Deirdre Coles.

This performance took place in January 1942 under the directorship of Sergeant Max Strietzel, a survivor of Buchenwald concentration camp and a conductor/violinist in his own right. He later acted alongside Russian-born actor Peter Ustinov in *School for Scandal*. That performance of *Babes in the Wood* which Willy and his army recruits enjoyed included the talent of other refugee soldiers in the army: Cecil Aronowitz, G. Guttmann, Hans Geiger, H. Hirschfeld (no relation of Willy), S. Mark, H. Moses, W. Kornfeld, H. Adler, Fritz Lustig, H. Harpuder, H. Kruh, F. Taylor, M. Maschowski, A. Neustadt and W. Stiasny. Over a two-year period numerous shows were staged in Ilfracombe by the entertainment section. Their success largely depended not only on the talent of the artists but also the choreography. There were a number of artists and their wives who could design and paint scenery, as well as provide the special lighting effects. Private Gurschner worked on the stage settings, Pte P. Wiesner acted as the stage manager and Ptes Preszow, Gruen and Santoro produced the lighting effects. Hannah Musch, prima ballerina, choreographer and wife of Pte Wiesner, designed some of the costumes. Willy remembers with fondness performances by Nicolai Poliakoff, otherwise known as Coco the Clown from his time with Bertram Mills' circus:

Coco was one of the most memorable characters in the army in Ilfracombe at that time. He was originally from Russia. When he volunteered early in the war, the government did not know what to do with him so they put him with the alien Pioneers. And there he stayed, organising shows with Sgt Strietzel. He brought no end of pleasure to people locally and to our soldiers, boosting our morale in the middle of war time. This was very important.

The alien soldiers were something of a curiosity to the local Ilfracombe population, who used to come out on Sundays to watch their parade along the seafront.

In Ilfracombe we always seemed to be marching. On one particular Sunday, we were marching along the promenade and amongst our refugees there was a huge burly man. The army couldn't find a uniform large enough to fit him. For the first few days he marched with us in civilian clothes. That particular Sunday we overheard one of the locals say, 'Gosh these guys are good. They've caught a German already!' Of course, it was still a time of great fear in Britain that the country might be invaded, although such fears were subsiding because Hitler had decided to turn his attention to Russia and diverted his military resources to that front. Even so, for a moment, we were viewed as heroes by the locals for supposedly catching a German.

The local people of Ilfracombe were exceptionally welcoming towards the new soldiers, even if a little wary at first because they were originally of German nationality. The initial suspicion was grounded in the fact that local men had fought, or had memories of the bitter fighting against Germany in the First World War.

Once Willy had completed his training in Ilfracombe, he was posted to 165 Pioneer Corps Company with his friends Gerry, Joe, Franz, Kurt and Herbert. The company at that time was stationed at Arncott near Bicester.

We were really nothing more than a glorified labour unit. In 165 Company we were assigned to help the Royal Engineers. At the beginning we were doing a lot of building work: construction of roads, defence work, mixing concrete, excavating trenches and laying railway track and drainage. I eventually joined the kitchens. I was sent on a cookery course in Reading. After two weeks I passed out as a cook. I got 9d. extra a day in my army pay. This allowance carried on until the end of my army career. From Oxford we moved to Thame.

Football once again featured largely in Willy's life. When he joined 165 Company, one of the first things he did was to volunteer for the company football team. This brought light relief and fun after a day of hard manual work.

From Thame, Willy was transferred to 248 Company which was then stationed at the Royal Engineers depot at Catterick Camp in Yorkshire. For the first time since leaving Australia he was separated from his small group of friends, but it was here that he first met, and became a lifelong friend of, Berlin-born Geoffrey Perry (originally Horst Pinschewer). Little could either of them imagine then, as they chatted together in Catterick Camp, that at the end of the war Geoffrey would arrest the wartime traitor William Joyce (Lord Haw-Haw) in woods near Flensburg, north of Hamburg. His story is told in detail in his auto-biography *When Life Becomes History*. While at Catterick Camp Willy was engaged in manual work for the Royal Engineers. He also volunteered for kitchen duties which meant occasionally having the perk of extra rations. Never one to be idle, he spent every spare moment making the most of his time, including again playing for the company football team in Catterick Camp.

> Being in the football team turned out to give us some preferential treatment. We were sometimes given light work, and not always sent out on detachments. During our time off, our outings were usually to the nearby town of Darlington where we attended dances. That was our main entertainment. I had friends stationed in 69 Pioneer Corps Company in Darlington so I was able to visit them. We had a lot of fun, but we needed it. No one knew at that time what the war held for us, although we had every hope in Britain and the leadership of Winston Churchill.

It was while Willy was at Catterick Camp that news circulated suggesting refugees from Nazi oppression were to be given the opportunity to transfer into fighting units of the British army. It was now 1943. Willy saw his opportunity to fight the Nazis. He volunteered for the Royal Armoured Corps (RAC) but the move took around six months to materialise.

> I was glad to get out of the Pioneer Corps to do something constructive for the war effort. I always felt that I could do more for the defeat of Nazism if I left the Pioneer Corps for a fighting regiment. My original idea was to become a glider pilot but since I played a lot of football in the army and had injured my foot with a minor break, I would not be accepted. My other choice was the Royal Armoured Corps.

In the meantime, on 26 April 1943 Willy's Pioneer company (248 Coy) changed from being an alien to a British company, so the men were transferred to other alien Pioneer companies. Willy went to 88 Company,

units, including the Royal Marine Commandos for special missions abroad, often requiring their knowledge of German. These men, like Willy, were to be involved in the major campaigns of the war, including the Normandy landings on, or shortly after, D-Day. Others were parachuted with the pathfinders into Arnhem to prepare the landing zones ahead of the main incoming airborne forces. Many others were involved in the Rhine crossings and invasion of Germany. They fought in regiments alongside their British-born comrades and were readily accepted in spite of their original background. By now, with a few exceptions, all had anglicised their names to avoid being treated as traitors in case of capture by the Nazis. As it turned out, a significant number of these German-speaking refugees heroically lost their lives on the battlefields of France, Belgium, Holland and Germany. They are buried under their anglicised names in the Allied war cemeteries of France and Holland, or commemorated on war memorials where there was no known grave.

Most of Willy's friends and acquaintances from internment in Australia enlisted in the British forces, all of them starting their army career in the 'alien' Pioneer Corps. This included Rudy Karrell (Rudi Katz, b. Berlin) who was always attached to some section of entertainment. He served in 74 Company of the Pioneer Corps and at the end of the war transferred to intelligence work with the British Army of the Rhine (BAOR) acting as interpreter; then to T Force, Hamburg, in charge of civil labour. Peter Eden (Werner Engel, b. Breslau) worked with Willy in the kitchens in Australia as 'our famous tea-maker'. Peter won the fiercely competitive Bridge championship in the camp. He enlisted in the Pioneer Corps, trained in Ilfracombe, then served with 249 Company in Scotland. In 1942 he was transferred to the Royal Engineers, Halifax headquarters and eventually sailed from Scotland to North Africa, landing at Algiers with the 1st Army working with the explosives corps of the Royal Engineers. After North Africa, Peter served in Palestine until 1945. Willy was also friendly with Bryan Fenton (Feder) who transferred from the Pioneer Corps to 3 Troop of No. 10 Inter-Allied Commando. He was engaged in active front-line service in Holland and Germany, and was among a group of 3 Troopers who, on a reconnaissance mission, were the first to cross the river Maas. Willy also struck up a lifelong friendship with Jonny Fraser who was in 165 Company of the Pioneer Corps and who later transferred to the Royal Engineers.

On 26 August 1943 Willy formally transferred to the 55th Training Regiment in Farnborough, Hampshire, to start training as a tank driver in the Royal Armoured Corps.

> For me, this was the highlight of my career – kitted out in my black beret and badge of the Royal Armoured Corps. Then I realised I was doing something I always wanted to do. To my surprise, I found out that several of my best friends from Australia (Joe Milton and Gerry Moore) had also joined the Royal Armoured Corps. All of us met again in Farnborough. It was wonderful to be training together again. At the end of the training, they were posted to 22nd Armoured Brigade as driver operators. We were not the only refugees at Farnborough. There were other ex-refugees whom we had never met before, but we were always in a minority. We were with predominantly British men, unlike our time in the Pioneer Corps. I personally did not encounter any anti-Semitism in the Royal Armoured Corps. My British comrades knew my country of origin and it did not affect how they treated me. I was totally accepted as one of them – and that was it.

Farnborough was full of troops at this time, not being far from the garrison town of Aldershot. The local people were very welcoming and the men regularly attended dances, or the cinema or pubs. On arrival at the training centre they were asked what role they wanted within the Royal Armoured Corps: tank driver, wireless operator or gunner. Willy explains:

> I opted for tank driver. When we arrived, those of us with German names were required to change them to something more English. This was to protect our original identity because if we were captured by the Nazis during the fighting abroad, then we would be treated as traitors and shot, rather than as prisoners of war. I entered the training centre at Farnborough as Willy Hirschfeld and left as William Field. Some of our men were later captured in Normandy and Holland, and their change of

name saved their lives. They returned safely from POW camps after the war. During my time at Farnborough, once again I joined the football team.

Willy was issued with new army number 13046415. This was an extra safety precaution because all numbers which began with the prefix 1380 could be traced back to German refugees in the British army (Pioneer Corps) and that was a danger when fighting abroad if captured. Training at Farnborough was rigorous. It consisted of 'square bashing', radio operating, weaponry, tank driving and map reading. There was also a strict daily routine of physical exercise. The men had to be 100 per cent fit to be accepted into the RAC and that included the successful completion of a ten-mile route march in full kit in less than two hours. Willy also learned to drive a variety of vehicles:

> We started off learning to drive a 15cwt small lorry. I had had some experience of driving lorries occasionally in the factory in Bonn, but that didn't make it easier for me. We had to negotiate a huge field. It was actually quite difficult in the beginning because we had to change the gears. We had to 'double de-clutch' and that was the most difficult part. Driving a tank or lorry is different from a car. To double de-clutch, we had to put the clutch in, then into gear, give it a bit of a rev, put clutch in again and then into the next gear. I seemed to manage and after several weeks I was able to drive this 15cwt very well.

The next step for Willy was learning to drive a tank. Training took place on a Cromwell; a fast, manoeuvrable tank with a Rolls-Royce engine that could reach speeds of 40mph. Weighing nearly forty tons, it had a 75mm gun and two Besa machine guns. The turret was hydraulically operated enabling it to rotate quickly under fire.

> There is no steering wheel in a tank like in a car or other vehicles. Inside a Cromwell, the gear lever is in the middle of your legs. On the right and on the left there are sticks for steering. Pulling the left lever, the tank goes to the left; the right lever it moves to the right. That was the easy

part. Changing gear was the most difficult part to master. The training instructor gave his instructions to us through our earphones which we had to wear at all times whilst driving. The fun part of a tank is being able to drive over large objects and very rough ground. We practised first on the roughest of ground to get used to the difficult terrain. Once we had enough practice we went out onto certain roads around Farnborough.

Apart from tank training, Willy learned about weaponry: how to use a machine gun, how to dismantle, reassemble and shoot a Besa. Once this was perfected he went out onto the shooting ranges. It was necessary to learn all aspects of firing ammunition, including from a tank gun in case of emergency during front-line action. If the gunner became injured, it was essential survival strategy for the whole tank crew. 'It was also necessary,' says Willy, 'for all of us to become driver mechanics to be able to carry out basic repairs of our tanks in action.' One of the key roles of a tank driver was maintenance of his tank. Training on all aspects of tank maintenance was crucial:

> This involved a series of checks every day: the amount of petrol and oil levels in the gears. We were taught how to change the caterpillar tracks. This was an extremely important part because the tracks, which are in sections, become loose over time and need tightening. We were all taught how to do this quite complicated task.

As the later official war diaries show, a good part of the time on active service was spent maintaining and repairing the tanks for the next operation. With the training finally completed, there was the passing out. This meant driving into the country with an instructor and an officer, and given instructions on where to drive: 'The passing out test lasted quite a long time and when I finished the officer said to me: "Trooper Field you did very well. You passed your test. You are now officially a tank driver."'

Next came the posting. Willy was sent to West Toft camp near Kings Lynn in Norfolk. He was to join C Squadron of the 8th King's Royal Irish Hussars. In total, over 216 refugees joined the Royal Armoured Corps, many of them drafted into the 8th King's Royal Irish Hussars

(8th Hussars) which was part of the 7th Armoured Division, famously named the Desert Rats after the emblem of the desert rat portrayed on their shoulder flash. They had suffered heavy casualties in the North African desert in 1942. The division had been engaged in fierce fighting against Rommel in Egypt and Tripoli. Eventually, Montgomery was appointed by Churchill and brought the first victories at El Alamein, Tripoli and Benghazi. The Axis powers had pushed the British forces back to Cairo. Morale was low and news of a victory was desperately needed to boost fighting spirits once again.

After Egypt, the Desert Rats were involved in the invasion of Sicily and Italy in the summer of 1943. They returned to England heavily depleted and in need of reinforcements for their next campaign. This may explain why so many German and Austrian refugees like Willy were assigned to the RAC regiments. Willy felt great pride in being part of the 8th Hussars:

> It was really how I expected the army to be. On our arrival at West Toft, our commanding officer explained a little bit about their recent campaigns abroad and what might be coming in the future, although exact details were still a State secret. I was now part of the famous Desert Rats and nothing could take away the feeling of exhilaration at being part of such a regiment. The first thing we did was to sew the emblem of the desert rat on our battledress and the green cord which we wore on our shoulder to distinguish ourselves as part of the 8th King's Royal Irish Hussars. Two weeks later our names were posted on the notice board with our roles. I was delighted to see my name as a tank driver and not a co-driver. It was a huge privilege and very exciting.

Each tank crew consisted of a commander, driver, a co-driver, gunner and wireless operator. Willy was allocated to C Squadron and waited to meet his fellow crew. The tank commander was Corporal Richards, the driver was Willy himself, Roy Rogers the co-driver, who was eventually replaced by John Sutherland, Albert Parfitt the gunner and John Gardner the wireless operator. Over the coming weeks they would become extremely close comrades. None were under any illusion of the possible dangers they faced – they were realistic about their future role out on the front line in Europe. They depended on each other for survival during action, thus it was essential that they learned to work together and look after each other. 'It was like being close family members but without the intense sibling rivalry,' comments Willy. The crew were given a Cromwell tank named *Carbine*. It was in *Carbine* that they went into action a few months later.

> I found the Cromwell a very fast tank, we were never happy with its gun. It wasn't really powerful enough – certainly not as powerful as the German 88mm and that is something we always regretted. The armour was adequate but again nothing like the German Panzer or Tiger tanks which we would be up against in battle. But, the beauty of the Cromwell was in its mobility. It could move very fast and change direction quickly and that would turn out to be its saving grace for us because it could save us from being knocked out in an attack.

Carbine was effectively to become their home in the coming months. They started intensive training together as a crew: 'We went out on tank exercises in the surrounding fields. We had to get to know each other to be able to work together in combat situations. We could well find ourselves dependent on each other for survival in wartime. We also had to learn how to do every member's job. As a crew we all actually got on very well.'

On 24 February the regiment received a special visit. Great excitement rippled through the camp at West Toft because the whole regiment was to be inspected by King George VI. That day is still a vivid memory for Willy:

> Given all that I had been through in recent years, it was an amazing moment to be inspected with my squadron by the King of England. He stopped by our tank and spoke to our commander Corporal Richards. Then he spoke to me and asked me 'what is your job?' I told him that I was the tank driver and that I also looked after the maintenance side of the tank. He showed a great interest. I felt very proud to

be part of all this. It gave me a sense of belonging. I had been rejected by my country of birth and now here I was serving the country which had saved my life.

Between February and April 1944, all squadrons of the 8th Hussars carried out further training and began extensive preparations for active service abroad. On 11 April, C Squadron moved to concentration areas for exercises with the 22nd Armoured Brigade. Later that day, Willy and other vehicle drivers left for Lowestoft for three days of practising wading tanks through water and driving them onto LCTs. On 14 April Willy's squadron carried out shooting practice at Titchwell. This was followed three days later with regimental training exercises in the Thetford and Stanford makeshift battle areas. Various levels of training continued until the end of the month when, on 27 April, the squadron made preparations to move.

By now all around Britain, British and American troops were preparing for Operation Overlord – the invasion of mainland Europe. At the end of April, heavy armoured vehicles and personnel began moving to secret locations in readiness for the next stage of the war. The troops knew that something was going to happen; that the invasion of Europe was imminent, but no details of the precise location were ever given. In the late afternoon of 29 April 1944, Willy's squadron moved their tanks by rail to Bognor Regis, a southern coastal town on the English Channel facing France. 'I remember loading our tanks onto the transport train,' he says. 'You had to be a good driver because it was tricky!' Ten Cromwell tanks were the first to be loaded onto transport trains, leaving at 1625 hours that day. They arrived at Bognor at 0105 hours on 30 April. Another seven tanks had left by rail at 2020 hours on the 29th, arriving at their destination at 0455 hours on the 30th. The final consignment of three tanks was moved at 1625 on 30 April, arriving at Bognor at 0105 hours on 1 May.

The men were billeted in Holyrood School in Bognor and in several hotels. Their tanks were parked in a local recreation ground. It was now crucial that their exact location was kept secret from friends and relatives; therefore their postal address was given as 'Army Post Office, England'.

On May Day that year, the men spent time settling into their new billets and carrying out maintenance on their vehicles:

Our billets in private houses and hotels on the seafront were very comfortable. The local people were very kind to us because they suspected what was going on. Seeing a large movement of troops to the coastal area of Southern England, it was not difficult to guess what was happening. We were always invited into their houses for tea and made extremely welcome. Our main entertainment in the evenings was a local pub called The Rising Sun. I knew very little about beer, but we certainly drank plenty of beer at that time – a beer called Tamplin which was brewed in Brighton. We got ourselves drunk quite a lot and enjoyed ourselves very much, but that was fine because we were not yet on invasion alert. We knew that things would happen to us eventually but in the meantime, we enjoyed ourselves.

On 4 May the vital task of waterproofing the vehicles and tanks began. This was essential for the invasion landings when most vehicles would be offloaded from the LCTs into shallow sea. Willy explains:

The waterproofing of our tanks took place over a couple of weeks. It was a busy time for us. Underneath the tanks there were loads of inspection plates which we had to unscrew, four screws on each. Each plate then had to be waterproofed by dipping it in special black glue to seal it. That was my job. The plates had to then be re-screwed onto the tank. It was hard work. The tank was raised on a platform and I worked under the tank for several hours at a time, dipping the inspection plates. We also fitted an extension onto our exhaust so that no water could get into the exhaust and cause our tanks to cut out. Once on dry land, the extension could be discarded. Having waterproofed the tanks, they then had to be tested in the water. We used to drive into the sea on Bognor seafront. It was quite a sight. This we did several times – and it was not always successful.

In the coming weeks, from 13–28 May, the regiment carried out a number of routine exercises, inspections and wading tests. The wading tests were conducted by driving the tanks into the sea to check they were waterproof: 'We were not happy until everything was okay and watertight. After all, our life and safety depended on it. It was the driver's responsibility to ensure its safety.'

The men also attended lectures on landscape and country terrain, as well as how to prepare and cook food on a primus stove which was supplied with every tank. Then at 0900 hours on 28 May 1944, the regiment received orders that they were on six hours notice to move. The entry in the official war diary for that day records:

> The Quartermaster will arrange to hold Rum on the scale of two tots per man, to be readily available for issue. After landing all personnel will be fed initially on compo pack rations. All vehicles will embark with tanks 90% full, in addition will carry Jerry cans of petrol for use only in an emergency. All tanks will have tarpaulin shelters and camouflage equipment. Soap will be issued on scale of 2oz per man for 14 days. Boot repairs will be carried out by trained personnel in the unit until local contracts can be made. Battle dress is to be worn.

On 5 June the regiment moved to Gosport where, at the signal, the vehicles would be loaded onto LCTs. They rested in a suburb of Gosport and waited. Due to bad weather, D-Day had been postponed from 5 June until 6 June. Once again, Willy and his crew found the local people welcoming. While they sojourned with their tanks in the street, a local lady came out and offered them a meal. Her husband was a captain serving in the war at sea, and she was only too pleased to offer the men hospitality. 'With her limited rations,' says Willy, 'she made us the most wonderful meal that I will never forget. It is memories like these which stay with you for a lifetime.'

In the early hours of 6 June 1944, the signal went up for the start of D-Day. Elements of the invasion force moved in large heavy convoys towards their ports of embarkation. Through the streets, the tanks made their slow move. The air was full of anticipation, excitement and fear. Women waved from windows and cheered them on their way. Willy was about to be part of the largest invasion force ever to land in Europe.

At that time we had a feeling that we were going somewhere, probably France, but no one told us exactly. It was exciting in a way – I felt it was an adventure. I felt no fear, neither was I nervous of going into action because this is what I had volunteered for and had been trained. I was ready to go into action and face whatever lay in store. None of us were under any illusion that this would be easy but at last, I felt that I had achieved something – I could take an active part in the war and do my bit towards the defeat of Hitler. I was doing something worthwhile towards the liberation of Europe from Nazi tyranny.

CHAPTER 6

D-DAY AND INTO BATTLE

On 6 June 1944 the colossal invasion force of Allied troops began their landings in Normandy. No one knew what lay ahead. Success was not assured, but with the strong leadership and moral fortitude of British Prime Minister Winston Churchill, there was optimism that the first phase of the liberation of Europe was under way.

Casualties and fatalities were high among the first wave of men who were parachuted into France just hours before D-Day to guide the incoming forces. Those who landed on D-Day itself and over the next couple of days faced stiff resistance from the enemy, with the highest fatalities suffered by the American forces that landed on Omaha beach. The various tank regiments landed in a continuous stream onto the beaches of Normandy. The 1st Royal Tank Regiment and A Squadron of the 8th Hussars landed D-Day+1. Ferocious fighting with much bloodshed had occurred the previous day, but they still encountered resistance and attacks from snipers. Between 6 and 9 June, Willy's squadron was waiting in Gosport for instructions to move. Then orders came to load the tanks onto the landing craft. It was a major operation, but one for which Willy and his team had prepared. Orders received, Willy drove his tank *Carbine* onto the LCT:

I recall we waited in the water for quite some time before we set off. During this time we had barrage balloons overhead for our protection, which were designed to ascend at great height, trailing fine steel wires to the ground to wreck any hostile airplanes. It was effectively an important defence against enemy aircraft. When we eventually set sail across the English Channel, the crossing was very rough. It was quite slow but an exciting crossing. We heard guns and bombs going off as we approached the coast of France, but it didn't worry us. During the crossing we sat on the top of our tanks, not inside. We could see what was happening ahead.

Willy's squadron landed on the beach near Arromanches on the Normandy coast on 9 June 1944, D-Day+3. For his squadron it turned out to be a straightforward landing:

We went through a certain amount of water, not too deep but one or two tanks managed to get stuck, not ours. The Royal Engineers were on hand to pull them out. We heard a bit of fire here and there but on the whole the landing was quite peaceful for us. Our first impression of the beaches – we saw a lot of broken tanks and gun installations. We could see that a fierce battle had taken place in the two days before we landed. The dead and wounded had been moved by this time.

Official war diaries record that C Squadron landed without casualties. They then moved inland towards Briquessard, south of Bayeux. The first phase, the Normandy landing, was over but months of bitter front-line fighting lay ahead in close cooperation with infantry regiments and sometimes Commando units.

The Normandy countryside proved to be the next major challenge. It was divided sharply between the 'campagne' and the 'bocage', with a narrow strip of marshland along the seashore. The newly landed forces had to move through 'campagne' territory which consisted of open, rolling plains mainly under crops, interspersed with occasional wooded valleys. To the south and west of Bayeux, the tank squadrons had to face the hazardous 'bocage' terrain with its maze of fields and orchards, surrounded by high-banked hedgerows. These hedgerows proved to be problematic because German snipers and anti-tank guns hid in them, targeting Allied tanks at ranges as close as 50 yards. The bocage was least penetrable south-east of Caumont towards Aunay-sur-Odon and the Orne valley.

The prime target for Allied forces, including the 8th Hussars, was the capture of Caen. To advance on Caen, it was necessary to push through the difficult bocage territory, via Briquessard. Having landed, Willy's squadron headed towards Briquessard where regimental headquarters had been set up. He recalls their first night:

Our tanks were all lined up against hedges so that we could not be seen. During the night German fighter planes, we called them 'shufti' planes, flew all over our tanks to try and identify us. For some reason they didn't fire at us but it was possible to just make out the pilot in the planes. We dived under our tanks for cover. During that first night we slept under our tank, something which we were forbidden to do again. This was because the tanks gradually sank into the earth. The next morning we found it hard to crawl out from underneath. We were lucky because we could have been crushed by the tank. After that we always slept out in the open beside our tanks. We had no canvas shelter, only blankets to keep warm.

On 12 June, the day that Winston Churchill visited General Montgomery in Normandy, the 8th Hussars moved to Briquessard via steep and narrow country lanes through the villages of Trungy, St Paul du Vernay, La Miere, Livry and finally into Briquessard itself. The 8th Hussars worked closely with units of the 22nd Armoured Brigade which consisted of a troop of 4th Field Squadron, Royal Engineers, 5th Royal Horse Artillery, 5th Royal Tank Regiment, infantry and two companies of the Rifle Brigade. The village of Livry was still held by the enemy, such that on 13 June with considerable activity the Germans defended their positions. German forces made constant attempts to probe Allied defences with their infantry placed in the hedgerows. During the three days and two nights in the area of Briquessard, C Squadron had to fight to survive; unfortunately they did lose one officer, Lt H.R.D. Pegler. The entry in the war diaries for 15 June 1944 records that: 'C Squadron was involved in close and confused fighting but all attacks were beaten off. Lt. H.R.D. Pegler was killed during the night.'

The following day was spent repairing damaged vehicles and recovering two tanks of A Squadron. During that time, C Squadron suffered numerous attacks but managed to beat off the enemy. The war diary entry for 17 June states that: 'C Squadron was attacked almost continuously during the night of 16/17 and by the morning of the 17th was very tired having been in their tanks for three days.' It was during this period that the squadron lost five tanks with eight personnel killed or missing. The war diaries then record that the squadron supported 1/6 Queens (infantry) to good effect, and it was largely due to them that forward position was held and a large number of the enemy killed. The grim and unexpected realities of war were all around them:

I always kept the visor of my tank open. I could see everything in front of me: the land, gun battles, dead animals lying all over the place, including masses of dead horses which the Germans had for transport. The stench of dead cows, sheep and horses was absolutely unbelievable when the wind was blowing in our direction. It smelt of foul, rotting flesh but, however unpleasant, we had to get used to it.

At the time Pegler was killed, an incident occurred with Willy and two other tanks which nearly cost them their lives. It highlights the dangers of advancing towards enemy positions:

We reached one spot in the Briquessard region where we had to stop behind hedges. We waited there all day and all night for something to happen. We were then told over the radio that we had advanced too far, too quickly, and should return immediately because we were in great danger. It was getting dark and I discovered that I couldn't start the tank because the wireless was continuously in operation and we were waiting for further instruction. I didn't dare start the tank because the battery was low and I wouldn't be able to keep in contact with headquarters. Then another of our tanks pushed me over the hedge right into the enemy lines about 20–30 yards so that I could start my tank. Luckily nothing happened. It was pitch dark and I was going very slowly. We couldn't put on our headlights, so we didn't know where we were going in the pitch dark of night. Fortunately, after 4–5 kilometres we reached our resting destination and safety. During this period of fighting, we became very tired because we were in our tanks continuously for two or three days without much sleep. We also lost quite a few tanks and that affected us.

When Willy and the crew finally returned to base, they were thoroughly exhausted. They lined their tanks up in a field of cows and, for the first time since they landed, had a ready supply of fresh milk (see plate 22: Willy and his mates milking the cows, tanks in the background). During his time on the front line, Willy was in charge of the food and cooking for his tank crew. Equipment was primitive but adequate:

We were given compo boxes which were wooden boxes containing certain foods: tea, milk powder, corned beef or Spam. There were also certain vegetables like beans, chocolate and cigarettes. Sometimes we were lucky to have a tin of peaches which we always kept for a purpose when we wanted to celebrate. For cooking we used a little primus stove and mess tins. We boiled water on this primus stove to make tea, and we could use it to reheat beans or soup. It was only a little tiny stove but it was adequate enough for our needs. During battle conditions we ate whenever we had a chance. When we were not fighting we ate in the army field kitchens. In terms of basics, whilst on the move, there were no toilets. We had to walk a few hundred yards from our tanks and dig a hole with a shovel. Whenever we could, we boiled hot water for a shave and wash. Personal hygiene was important for us. Once back at regimental headquarters we used showers. Supplies of fresh water for drinking and cooking, and petrol for the tanks, were delivered to us by lorry.

One day, in the region of Briquessard, Willy unexpectedly met a friend from his Pioneer Corps days, also an ex-German Jewish refugee. He was Henry Hall (originally Heinz Halm). He had been with Willy in

248 Company and 88 Company of the Pioneer Corps, and also trained at Farnborough. Henry became a wireless operator and served in the 1st Battalion, Royal Tank Regiment. Little could Willy have imagined then that he would see Henry on the battlefields of France:

> Somewhere near Briquessard, the 8th Hussars were relieved by the 1st Battalion, Royal Tank Regiment. I saw my friend Henry Hall with his tank crew. He was now co-driver of a Sherman tank. We had time to chat for about ten minutes and that was the last I saw of him until after my demobb. Then after the war, I was going to see a Cary Grant film at the cinema in Marble Arch, London. I was with my old army friend Joe Milton. Suddenly, Henry Hall walked passed us. We recognised each other and he joined us in the queue for the film. He told us that shortly after I had seen him in Normandy he was wounded in action during German shelling. He was hit by shrapnel and had to be flown back to England where he underwent an operation. That was the end of the war for him. Later I was best man at his wedding and we are still good friends to this day.

Back to Normandy 1944, and making small advances through the bocage took weeks for the infantry and the different tank regiments, including the 8th Hussars, 5th Royal Tanks and 1st Royal Tank Regiment. Mont Pinçon became one of the main objectives because its summit had a ridge from which the surrounding region could be surveyed. In the end, it turned out not to be as useful strategically as Allied forces had hoped. Over the next three weeks the troops found themselves in an uneasy stalemate of fighting in the bocage, with enemy sniping, shelling and mortaring. The only news of the outside world which Willy and his comrades received was when they were at headquarters on rest and maintenance, or otherwise from the lorry drivers who brought supplies of petrol, food and water to them near the front line. The men were isolated from everything except the immediate war around them. Willy's squadron advanced further east, returning to regimental headquarters periodically for rest and maintenance. It was while they were resting somewhere in this region that Willy nearly lost his life:

I had a good friend called Jimmy who was driver of a Churchill tank in C Squadron of the 8th Hussars. He was a Cockney who was always wheeling and dealing in some scheme. He was quite a character and would keep an eye out for any loot from abandoned German military vehicles. He acquired, for example, well-made German binoculars and a Luger (gun). One day he asked me to go with him over to a broken-down German lorry. I declined saying that I desperately needed the toilet. Apart from that, I did not share his enthusiasm for abandoned goods. The lorry was but 50–60 yards away. He insisted that I went over with him. I took one glance back at the toilet block, which were primitive huts, and said, 'Okay, but just this once.' Whilst we were stood by the German lorry a shell landed right on the toilet hut and completely destroyed it. I stared in disbelief. If I had gone to the toilet, I would have been dead. That day, quite by chance, Jimmy saved my life.

On 19 June Willy's squadron was ordered back to La Butte where regimental headquarters was then based. A few days later on 23 June, they were given lectures and briefings on the progress of the war. At 6.30 a.m. on 26 June, Willy and his tank crew were on the move again. As they advanced, their targets included attacks on known enemy positions in hedgerows and along railway lines in order to root out German guns which had been installed there to disrupt supply lines. On 2 July C Squadron relieved B Squadron, with little enemy activity. They maintained patrols up until last light. Two days later on 4 July, the regiment moved to the area of Condé-sur-Seulles, south-east of Bayeux.

On 6 July all squadrons were at two hours notice for the next move. In the meantime they received training on map reading, tactical movement and mine detection. On 10 July they carried out training with infantry units. The 8th Hussars eventually advanced on Caen. The area of Villers-Bocage to the east would see some of the fiercest fighting, with stiff resistance from German SS Panzer divisions. Willy comments:

The German Tiger and Panther tanks were much bigger and heavier armoured than our tanks. They had 88mm guns which were extremely powerful, but their turrets were fixed making it not so easy to change direction to shoot their target. They had to move the whole tank to line up their guns. They could not manoeuvre as fast as we could – and that was our greatest advantage during the war. On one occasion my commanding officer shouted: 'Get out of his way. There's a f—g Tiger coming towards us. Turn!' I turned as quick as I could and we got away. We were out of his direct range of fire. That, for me, demonstrated the benefits of the Cromwell tank.

On 13 July C Squadron carried out operational training with 1/6 Queens Infantry. Preparations were under way for the next phase: crossing the River Orne. At 0900 hours on 17 July the whole regiment was formed up ready to move, now based in orchards around Jerusalem, a few miles south of Condé-sur-Seulles. The 6th Airborne Division had already captured the bridgehead over the Orne. At ten o'clock the following day the 8th King's Royal Irish Hussars moved out on the approach march to the Orne bridgehead, Pegasus Bridge. Official war diaries record that: 'After a slow start and many hold-ups, the order was reacted circa 2200 hours, but the Regiment was unable to cross.' This was due in part to enemy activity. Some infantry divisions had managed to cross, but the scene which faced Willy and his comrades in the 8th Hussars is described in the official regimental history:

> The Division moved across the Orne in blinding dust, and the degree of traffic congestion which was to be expected from the movement of two armoured divisions on a narrow front. That night we had our first taste of the Luftwaffe deployed in strength, which, although not numerous by RAF standards, was able to make life on the bridges very unpleasant for those crossing and for the traffic control personnel.

On 19 July the regiment had crossed the Orne and leaguered in the area of Giberville. They proceeded to Bourguebus, south of Caen, and next day was in support of 131 Brigade in that area. By early evening, C Squadron had moved into the Soliers area, occupying positions of observation in the village. Willy comments:

1 Arthur Hirschfeld (front row, second on the right – with the pipe) with his infantry regiment in the First World War.

2 Willy and twin sister Thea with elder sister Betty, Bonn.

3 The Hirschfeld house, 14 Lenné Strasse, Bonn, with sister Thea looking out of the window.

4 Arthur Hirschfeld on holiday in Knokke, Belgium, 1927.

5 The Hirschfeld extended family, Bonn, 1930. Willy is standing at the back on the left, next to his father.

6 Willy in gymnastics class at the Jewish school in Bonn, 1935. Willy is the boy upside down between the chairs.

7 With the family on the Rhine, 1925.

8 Arthur Hirschfeld's shop, Gangolfstrasse, Bonn, 1926.

9 Remigius Strasse, Bonn, 1935.

10 Wolfstrasse, Bonn under the Nazis, 1935.

11 The factory where Willy was arrested on *Kristallnacht*, 10 November 1938.

12 Ledger entry for Willy's arrival in Dachau concentration camp, 15 November 1938.

13 Willy with his family just after his release from Dachau concentration camp.
Willy is standing at the back on the right-hand side.

14 Pencil sketch of Willy by artist
Robert Hofmann on the *Dunera*,
dated 4 August 1940.

H.M.T.S. „DUNERA"
August 4ᵗᵉ
Robert Hofmann

15 Ilfracombe, North Devon, where Willy and other refugees trained in the British
army's Pioneer Corps.

16 Willy when he joined the Pioneer Corps, Ilfracombe, 1941.

17 Willy with 248 Company, Pioneer Corps at Catterick Camp, Yorkshire.

18 C Squadron, 8th King's Royal Irish Hussars, landing near Arromanches on D-Day+3.

19 C Squadron, 8th King's Royal Irish Hussars, D-Day+3.

20 Willy with C Squadron, 8th King's Royal Irish Hussars, unloading tanks from the LCT onto the beaches of Normandy.

21 Willy (middle row, third from left) with his tank *Carbine* and original crew taking a break in the fields of Normandy, near Briquessard, June 1944.

22 Willy with his tank crew milking cows during a rest in fields in Normandy, June 1944.

23 Knocked out German tank in France, June 1944.

24 The 8th King's Royal Irish Hussars with 1 Commando Brigade charging towards the village of Linne in Holland, January 1945. (Drawing by Brian de Grinean)

25 Willy in the 8th King's Royal Irish Hussars, Lingen, Germany, 1946.

26 Twin sister Thea in the ATS, 1944/5.

27 A tank crew of the 8th King's Royal Irish Hussars with captured Nazi flag, en route to Hamburg, April 1945. Willy is seated far right (above the eagle insignia).

28 Willy with his tank at the Victory Parade, Berlin, July 1945.

29 The Reichstag (parliament), Berlin, July 1945.

30 Willy with his comrades outside Hamburg, 1945.

31 Willy driving lead tank of the 7th Armoured Division into Berlin, July 1945, behind an armoured car.

32 Visiting Hitler's bunker, Berlin, July 1945.

33 The Victory Parade, Berlin, 21 July 1945.

34 Marriage to Judy (Jutta) Fabian, 29 March 1949.

35 Willy at Arsenal's Emirates Stadium.

During the days of our advance on Caen, I was called upon to interrogate German POWs because my native tongue was German. I asked them where they had been and about their instructions. I had to then interpret for the POWs in the responses. By now they were ready to talk. They were fed up with the war and were pleased to be taken prisoner because it meant the war was over for them. Most of them were fairly young soldiers. When I spoke to the first German prisoners it was exciting in a way. I was not angry in spite of all that I had been through. It's not in my nature to harbour resentment or anger. Winning the war was good enough for me.

Between 20–24 July, the Normandy campaign had reached something of a stalemate. No progress was being made in the advance and defensive positions were held by Allied forces. But during this period, German units were able to bring up reinforcements. On 21 July A and C Squadrons were able to observe enemy movements and dispositions on their fronts. Some enemy tanks were seen and targets were found for 5 Royal Horse Artillery who carried out effective barrages. Both squadrons suffered fairly heavy and accurate shellfire during the day, resulting in the death of Lt D.S. Scott. Willy remembers it well:

Another officer of ours was killed in action, his name was Lieutenant Scott. He was our Troop leader, killed by a German sniper when he looked out of the tank. He was a wonderful man and very much liked by us.

Scott is buried in Ranville war cemetery.

The following day, A and C Squadrons observed enemy positions. Shelling continued by day and several casualties were sustained. B Squadron then relieved C Squadron and C Squadron returned to regimental headquarters. They were able to watch the RAF bombardment of Caen:

Caen was completely flattened by the RAF. When we drove our tanks through after the major battles on the ground, the town was a massive pile of rubble and dust with very little still standing. Looking at the utter devastation, it seemed like something out of the Apocalypse.

The war diary entry for 24 July 1944 records that the commanding officer ordered the start of Operation Spring and put all ranks in the general picture, telling them the overall plan and role of the regiment. At 6 a.m. the following day the regiment was formed up ready to move. The route was 082656 – 054672 – 042661 – 047644 where the regiment halted and deployed off the road. C Squadron went to area 045642. Squadron Major G.W.G. Threlfall MC was killed by a shell bursting close to his tank while he was outside it. He too is buried in the Ranville war cemetery. Captain Ames took over command of the squadron.

By now, the regiment was moving from Bourguebus to Tilly-la-Campagne to May-sur-Orne. Enemy tanks and infantry were well dug in and progress was slow. On 26 July C Squadron leaguered at regimental headquarters at Verrières, coming under shellfire that forced them to spend the rest of the day in tanks or slit trenches. On the far bank of the Orne, the enemy had five Panzer or SS Panzer divisions and artillery which were supported by night bombers. Some of C Squadron tanks were dug in by an armoured bulldozer. They were shelled again the following day. On 28 July a troop of C Squadron was engaged at a factory south of Verrières and regimental headquarters came under heavy enemy shellfire. The move to the west of the Orne began over the next two days under continued enemy shelling, while the enemy sustained heavy casualties from RAF bombing. A stalemate was reached in the fighting and the official regimental history recorded:

> It would not be an exaggeration to say that the tank fighting on the Caen sector, however fruitless it might have appeared at the time, had a decisive effect on the battle of the bridgehead in that it forced a vital delay on any plans to concentrate the German armour to meet the American threats.

The Americans were concentrating on an advance from the Cherbourg Peninsula. On 30 July the regiment completed a difficult night march back to the bocage country, south of Bayeux, and harboured in area Abbaye du Mondaye, arriving at 7.30 a.m. They rested in a field and spent the day on maintenance and refitting for future operations. The bocage area was a welcome break from the dust and mud of the Caen plains.

On 1 August 1944 the regiment was on the move again. This time the route was via the Caumont-By-Pass to Cahagnes, to crossroads at Robin to Jurques, then Mesnil Azouf and finally Mont Pinçon. Progress was slow. By the last night regimental HQ had reached Cahagnes. During the night they were attacked by enemy aircraft and sustained casualties. Meanwhile, the infantry were still clearing enemy positions on the main road and around Briquessard, the enemy being protected by mines, tanks and anti-tank guns. Heavy casualties were suffered by 1/6 Queens.

On 3 August C Squadron took ten POWs. On 4 August they observed enemy activity and then the regiment advanced to Aunay-sur-Odon, which they found in ruins from Allied bombing. The route was planned from Robin to St Georges d'Aunay to Longvillers. The next five days were spent pushing forwards. It was a tough advance. The 8th Hussars came up against many mines, anti-tank guns and bazookas. Dry and dusty roads alerted enemy observation posts to any movement on them. By 5 August Germans began withdrawing from positions west of the Orne. On 8 August C Squadron was guarding the crossroads at Vallée. Regimental HQ took four enemy deserters who emerged from the woods.

From 9–10 August C Squadron moved into reserve. At 9.30 a.m. on 11 August, all officers and NCOs attended a talk by Lieutenant-General Horrocks, commander of XXX Corps. He spoke of the achievements of the division, of the progress of the war and his pleasure at having the division under his command. The rest of the day was observed as a holiday. The war diaries record that the men went for a bath, attended cinema and ENSA shows. For Willy, it proved to be a memorable day:

In Vallée, we lined our tanks up outside the house where we were billeted. We were completely filthy from the recent fighting. The only occupant of the house was an elderly lady and I could make myself understood by speaking a little German to her. All males in the village had been taken away by the Germans to forced labour camps. She took pity on me. 'I will get a bath ready for you,' she told me. An hour later, she called me into the kitchen. There in front of me was a tin bath full of warm water. She left the room and I relaxed in the bath. It was only four to five minutes before the door opened and in walked a visiting general, my squadron leader and sergeant major. My immediate reaction was to stand up and salute them. I got up and stood stark naked before them, saluting! My squadron leader just said, 'Carry on, Field.' With that, they left.

Between 12 and 15 August the regiment carried out maintenance and recreation in preparation for the next stage of the advance. By 14 August the enemy was still in retreat, now east towards the Seine through Falaise. The regimental break, almost a holiday, was cut short to begin the break-through and the capture of Lisieux and the advance on the Seine. Orders were received on 15 August to move from Hamars to St Sylvian. The following day the regiment headed towards St Pierre-sur-Dives. The scene is well described in the official regimental history:

> ... the Division was concentrated in a crowded and dusty area, well lit-
> tered with the debris of war, 'brewed' tanks and vehicles, dead cattle,
> abandoned guns and a number of unburied corpses. The journey across
> had been long and slow, through clouds of dust and through some of the
> worst areas of the Normandy fighting. May-sur-Orne, where we crossed
> a bridge over the river, was once a pleasant stone village, sheltered by the
> steep wooded banks of the Orne River, and surrounded by deep, rich pas-
> tures and meadows. It was now a mass of rubble, its trees broken, stripped
> of [their] leaves, its riches rotting among the bomb craters. That night
> and the following one were also made unpleasant, though not particularly
> dangerous, by the Luftwaffe. Destruction, as an ever-present companion
> to war, was soon to be left behind.

On 17 August B and C Squadrons met stiff opposition east of St Pierre-sur-Dives. One tank of C Squadron was knocked out by a bazooka. They faced the remnants of enemy in retreat from 12th SS and 21st Panzer Divisions. Around St Pierre, the terrain of rolling cornfields was in marked contrast to the bocage country. Beyond the river valley resembled the bocage with small orchards and woods.

On 18 August the regiment advanced on Livarot. The route was Boissey (a village in the valley), La Saminiere and finally Livarot. In the area of La Saminier, C Squadron met anti-tank guns which knocked out the leading tank of 5 Troop. Subsequently, 3 Troop took the lead but also had its leading tank knocked out. The anti-tank gun was then blown out by the troop leader, but his tank was hit by another gun. He was killed. The war diary entry for that day records an accident by friendly fire: 'Throughout the afternoon casualties and damage were caused to our troops by the attacks of our own fighter aircraft and the intelligence officer was badly wounded.' Willy recalls:

> It was a difficult period. In this area every bend concealed a German Tiger, Panther or anti-tank gun. Enemy infantry were also strategically hidden to attack us. It was hard for us to advance at times because every bridge and culvert had been blown and in places the roads were cratered.

The 8th Hussars with 1/6 and 1/7 Queens reached the plateau over-looking Livarot. Patrols of the 8th Hussars found an unguarded bridge intact and were able to cross the River Vie with the 1st Rifle Brigade. On 19 August Willy's squadron retired into reserve. Two days later rein-forcements arrived from the Northants Yeomanry. The Royal Engineers completed the construction of a bridge at Livarot and thus the libera-tion of Livarot followed which was described in the official regimental history as 'welcome, restrained but genuine'. It went on to say that 'here for the first time we met the Resistance movement which provided us with good information, and also handed over a number of allied airmen … The battle for Livarot had not been easy. It had taken three days to cover nine miles from St Pierre and daily casualties were some forty to fifty men.'

The push then continued from St Jacques to St Georges du Vièvre, en route to Pont Authou. On 26 August the regiment advanced towards Pont Authou and crossed the River Risle. At four o'clock that afternoon, B and C Squadrons sent patrols out to the area of Bosc-Renoult with the aim of leading the enemy to believe that the advance was continuing on Routot. The following day the war diaries record that: 'C Squadron headed to the line of Northings 05 (Bosc-Renoult), then halted to wait for B Squadron. C Squadron moved from Bourg-Achard to Routot.

One tank knocked out, crew survived.' The whole regiment then moved back to a new divisional area at Lieurey. The following day it moved towards Louviers, west of the Seine, on a route through Lieurey to Giverville and Fontaine. The ultimate aim was to cross the River Seine, a military necessity. The various troops waited to cross, on the verge of yet another momentous breakthrough. By now, the vital battles in France were behind them. They had achieved remarkable success in less than three months since D-Day. The official regimental history records: 'at the time it was hard to believe that the Battle for France was now virtually over, for the enemy still appeared to have plenty of fight left in him, but the final move to complete a decisive victory was now drawing near.'

All focus now centred on the next major objective of the war – the capture of Ghent in Belgium. In the immediate future, this meant crossing the River Seine. On 31 August the regiment headed for the Seine, but their crossing was delayed by bridge repairs being carried out by the Royal Engineers. Movement was extremely slow on the congested roads. The sheer volume of vehicles waiting to cross was extraordinary. Progress was slowed further by the fact that only one bridge over the Seine was strong enough to bear the weight of a tank.

The next phase of the war was one in which the forces felt well prepared. The advance on Ghent would be carried out on quieter roads, and through villages and towns relatively undamaged by war. There was still fighting to be done, but the Royal Armoured Corps was prepared. The enemy's disintegration on the front was in evidence as the tanks and infantry pushed forwards. The terrain was characterised by woods, areas of hedged fields and orchards. On 1 September Willy's squadron crossed the River Somme, the scene of so much suffering, trench warfare and high casualties during the First World War. Those lasting images must have affected the men fighting in the region just over twenty years later:

> When we approached for the crossing of the Somme, we were aware of being in the region of the most terrible battles from the First World War. How could we forget the images of mud and slaughter of millions of men? I thought of my father fighting on the German side against Britain

back then. He had fought at the Battle of Verdun. It was the only thing he ever said about the war: the mud and Battle of Verdun; otherwise he just didn't talk about it.

On 2 September C Squadron came into contact with the enemy south of St Pôl. The town of Frevent was strongly held with an anti-tank gun on the main road. They faced an extremely difficult battle. Two C Squadron tanks attempting to force a passage were knocked out. That same day Willy lost another comrade in battle, this time his friend and fellow-refugee Trooper Ernest Hugh Jacoby:

> I was quite friendly with him because he was in the same squadron as me. I remember at the time he was driving an officer who was second-in-command and his tank was usually behind in what is called the rear flank tank. He suddenly drove past my tank to pick up wounded soldiers. He was on this tank when he was hit and killed trying to rescue the injured. I still have a very clear picture of him lying on his own tank, dead. He was returned to us, together with the other wounded soldiers.

Jacoby is buried at the London cemetery, Longueval in France.

The following day St Pôl was still stubbornly held by the enemy. Orders were given to C Company of 1/7 Queens to enter the town and secure it for Allied forces. One squadron leader of C Squadron, 8th Hussars, was severely wounded by shrapnel, but otherwise casualties at this time were light. A number of POWs were taken. On 4 September Willy's squadron received orders to move through Duneville to Ternas. The following day was spent on maintenance of tanks and vehicles and much-needed rest. However, heavy rain hampered the vital maintenance work. The low ground became so boggy that a reconnaissance party was sent to a nearby village to look for billets. On 7 September the men were moved into the village of Cambligneul, and by 8 September they had moved on to Hersin where hot showers were organised in the town.

The enemy seemed ready to surrender near Audenarde on the River Scheldt on which the city of Ghent stands. Local civilians reported that the enemy was now positioned south and south-west of Ghent. The terrain was markedly different now as described in the regimental history:

> It was flat going all the way along the poplar-lined roads, through the intensely cultivated, dyked fields of Flanders, the rich farms with their orchards, and the numerous ugly villages and hamlets … As if to compensate for the drabness of the landscape, the houses were decorated with enormous Belgian flags, and cheering, excited civilians lined the streets across which were draped suitable expressions of greeting.

Wherever the forces advanced through Belgium, they received a warm welcome from the local people. In the villages the troops were given baskets of tomatoes. It was one of the few offerings of friendship the Belgians could give at that time considering the wartime shortage of food. Willy fried the tomatoes for his crew every breakfast time, but soon the quantity became overwhelming: 'Every village we entered gave us baskets of them. It got to the stage where we stayed inside our tank so we weren't given any more tomatoes! I hate fried tomatoes to this day!'

Ghent was liberated by sections of the Allied forces on 6 September 1944. Willy was involved in that historic event:

> I took part in the liberation of Ghent – some of us were sent ahead of the main regiment. The houses had white bed sheets hanging out of the windows. The people were happy that we had arrived and greeted us like heroes. They too showered us with food, especially tomatoes. They must have suffered a great deal under the Nazis.

Leave parties began to visit neighbouring towns, war memorials and battlefields of the last war. This was followed by two days of maintenance and rest. Orders were received for the rest of the regiment to move and the following day, at around 11 a.m. on 11 September 1944, it crossed into Belgium, finally resting about one mile east of Oordegem.

CHAPTER 7

ADVANCE THROUGH BELGIUM AND HOLLAND

On the afternoon of 12 September 1944, after a day spent on refitting and maintenance, the 8th Hussars moved to an area east of Mâlines (Mechelen) in Belgium where the enemy did little except send out random artillery and mortar fire. The following day arrangements were made to send relief parties into Brussels. By now the 11th Hussars, also working in the region of the 8th Hussars, held a position watching the line of the Canal de Jonction between Antwerp and Lierre. The next objective was to push towards Holland and cross the border. On 15 September the regiment advanced towards Lierre and two days later heavy enemy mortar fire caused two casualties in C Squadron.

Orders were received for the next move. On 18 September, according to the war diaries, the regiment set off at 7.20 a.m. on a route from Lierre to Konings-Hooikt and Booischot. C Squadron was ordered to move to the area of Boekel. There was little enemy activity, although the Germans were still occupying Herentals. On 21 September orders were received to extend eastwards. The next day a troop from C Squadron came across four American airmen who had bailed out of their planes and evacuated them. Now Willy waited with the rest of C Squadron to advance on Eindhoven in Holland. On 24 September they were finally given orders to advance on Schijndel, situated north of Eindhoven and south of S'Hertogenbosch. C Squadron cleared woods en route and led the way on the main road. The war diaries record that the regiment 'captured an enemy ambulance, knocked out three enemy transports and two 88mm anti-tank guns'.

On 26 September patrols from C Squadron went forward to harass the enemy, overrunning several positions and taking fifteen German POWs. The war diaries record that 'the forward squadrons received heavy mortar and shellfire from the enemy, and several casualties caused'. One of those casualties was Willy. His tank received a direct hit and was knocked out. He describes that dreadful day in which he was the sole survivor of his crew:

> We were heading towards Nijmegen and told that we should take a railway line. My tank was the lead tank. It was never a good thing for us to be at the front, because naturally the life expectancy of a leading tank was always very short. We saw the railway line ahead of us from quite a long distance. We stopped next to a haystack and my commander said that he had seen some movement ahead in the bushes. He suggested that we stay put until we knew exactly what was happening ahead. The next thing we heard was the haystack receiving a trace of bullets from the Germans. It caught fire immediately. It was so hot and bad that we could not stay with our tank next to the haystack so we had to move. The next thing I can remember was the turret of my tank being hit by an 88mm gun from a German anti-tank gun [sic]. The tank filled with smoke and was on fire. I tried to get out of my driver's seat and went up to the turret. I could already see that my commander Corporal Richards and the gunner Albert Parfitt were dead, both badly burned. I didn't see the co-driver John Sutherland, and don't know what happened to him, but he definitely didn't survive. The wireless operator John Gardner was still in the turret. I managed to pull him out of the burning tank alive and put him safely behind it. He was really badly injured in the leg and arm.

Willy then climbed back into the tank. A second hit from an 88mm gun shot through the driver's seat, throwing him about 10–15 yards. He was wounded, with shrapnel lodged in his upper left thigh. He could barely walk. He shuffled his way back to Allied lines, a distance of about 300 yards where help was at hand. A medical team was sent forward for Gardner, but he died on the way to the first-aid station. By now, Willy's knocked-out tank *Carbine* was burning and smoking.

Willy was taken by jeep to a nearby field hospital and then transported to a main hospital somewhere in Belgium where he remained for more than three weeks. He recalls:

> The only thing I remember about recovering in hospital is one particular nurse who insisted on giving me Ovalmatine [Ovaltine], a milky drink. I hated it. Otherwise I was very well treated. My wounds healed, but the shrapnel could not be removed and remains in my leg to this day.

For Willy, the shock of seeing his mates killed remained with him. The full trauma of it finally hit him when his commanding officer took him back to see the burned-out tank a few weeks later. When he saw the state of *Carbine*, he realised just how lucky he had been to survive that day. Later he learned that all his comrades were buried at the British military cemetery at Eindhoven. Trooper Albert Parfitt was twenty years old, John Sutherland aged thirty-one and John Gardner aged twenty-three.

Sometimes the small things in life have the greatest impact. One thing continues to disturb Willy regarding his crew. It has to do with tinned peaches:

> It was rare in wartime to have a tin of peaches in our compo boxes. One day, just before going into action, we received a compo box and were lucky that inside was a tin of peaches. The rest of my tank crew wanted to open it right away and dish them out, but I was determined that we should keep it for a time of celebration. After all, it was wartime and we should keep something for a special occasion. Unfortunately, when our tank was blown up near Nijmegen in that September of 1944, the tin of peaches went with it. My comrades all died and we never got to share

those peaches together. That is something I felt guilty about after their deaths. We should have enjoyed it at the time and not waited.

While Willy was in hospital recovering from his wounds, C Squadron had moved 10km north-west of Boekel to Veghel. By mid-October they were in and around Eindhoven, a city that had been heavily bombed by the Germans long before Allied troops got there. Reconnaissance patrols were sent out regularly and preparations made for forthcoming operations. Around this time Willy returned to his unit, initially based in Belgium with regimental headquarters looking after food and supplies. He eventually returned to front-line fighting with a new tank and crew, this time as driver for Captain Firth who was second-in-command of the squadron. He comments: 'Captain Firth was a good soldier. I liked him very much. He was very fair and had a great deal of understanding.'

During October, Willy received a moving letter dated 16 October 1944 from the parents of John Gardner, the last of his tank crew to be killed. It was written by Revd Gardner of St George's Presbyterian Church, Palmers Green in North London:

Major Huth has written to us telling us how our son Trooper J. A. Gardner met his death. He tells us that you got him out of the tank and went back for assistance. All I wish to do is to thank you on behalf of my wife and myself for all that you did for our son in his hour of great need. We are most grateful to you. We know you by name, for in some of his letters, John referred to your excellent powers of cooking. I need not say that this has been a crushing blow for us. We had hoped that our son would have been spared to the end and it is desolating to know that he is not coming back. We must bear our sorrow with the same courage and fortitude that he showed amid all the horrors of war. He was a very shy boy and I think his shyness hid his abilities. There was much in the army that he disliked, much that hurt his sensitive nature but he always spoke of the good comradeship of the men with whom he was; had it not been for that I don't know what he would have done. I do not know where you live, but if ever you are in London, I hope you will call upon us and allow us personally to thank you for what you did for one who was – and still is – very dear to us.

During his first army leave after front-line fighting had finished, Willy went to London and made it his priority to visit Revd and Mrs Gardner. It was an emotional occasion, as he himself recounts:

> For me, it was not an easy thing to tell John Gardner's parents that they had lost their son. Major Huth had already informed them officially, but of course I was one of the last people to see him alive. I could only tell them what a wonderful person he was and very much liked. I was able to explain that as far as I could tell, he did not suffer too long. This gave them some comfort, but I felt somewhat guilty standing in front of them because I had survived and their son had died. They were very kind to me that day. They had heard all about me from their son, and thanked me for helping him in his hour of need. I still have their letter in my possession to this day because it means so much to me. Sometimes I feel like reading it again, so I get it out and reflect on my comrades who died and how fortunate that, by chance, I survived. War is a terrible thing – it affects one deeply, especially the loss of our comrades in the fighting. That stays with you forever.

On 22 October 1944 the 8th Hussars lost more tanks while fighting in the region towards Berlicum. A few days later, on 26 October, it prepared to cross the Zuid Willems Canal and advance on Loon op Zand. On 27 October Willy's squadron lost two tanks from German anti-tank guns sited north of the main road towards Loon op Zand where they encountered stiff opposition. The following day they came under heavy fire and were forced to withdraw. On 1 November 1944, after much bitter fighting, the 8th Hussars moved to Sprang, opposite the enemy positioned north of the Maas river at the delta. Here the 8th Hussars received occasional shelling by the enemy.

The regiment then had to carry out vital maintenance work, which included fitting new tracks to the tanks. At 3.45 p.m. on 4 November, the squadrons moved into battle positions. Operations commenced and fires lit by the enemy were soon spotted on Aftwaterings Island. Some enemy deserters were taken prisoner. Willy recalls the state of the war at this time and his role with the German POWs:

By now pockets of the German army were fed up with endless marching and counter-marching. They could see that Allied troops were gradually forcing their retreat and so some surrendered. They had little food and rest and were thoroughly demoralised. They had no more will-power to fight. But that wasn't the full picture everywhere. We would soon be fighting die-hard Nazis who refused to give up their cause. I was often asked by my commander to speak to the POWs. The prisoners were always surprised when I spoke to them in proper German. Sometimes I was involved in interrogating them for intelligence purposes – finding out where they had been, what fighting they had been doing and where they were heading just before they were taken prisoner.

The 8th Hussars continued to send tanks and armoured cars out on reconnaissance patrols. The enemy's strategy was to gain time, to prevent Allied forces crossing the rivers which protected the frontiers of Germany, most notably the Rhine, before winter set in. If that could be delayed, then German forces could re-equip and build up defences over the winter. The terrain which the Allied forces now faced in Holland was generally cultivated land, interspersed with thick woods. Roads in the area were few and in poor condition, making progress slow at times for tanks and heavy vehicles. Fighting was persistent but not bitter. The enemy was prepared to withdraw under pressure, but not yet willing to abandon the western Netherlands.

On 6 November Willy moved with his squadron into Aftwaterings Island. The enemy had retreated and was now holding vital approaches to S'Hertogenbosch. The war diaries record that on 7 November the enemy was quiet. 'There wasn't much fighting here,' says Willy. 'Our tanks couldn't move much during the winter so we were holding the lines. We could often see the enemy positions in the far distance.'

Allied operations in the area were now concentrated on the next major task – crossing the River Maas before winter set in. It would be some time before this was accomplished. The immediate military strategy was to capture S'Hertogenbosch. The 8th Hussars with Divisional Artillery, 131 Brigade and 1st Royal Tanks was to clear the area of Middelrode, Doornhoek and Berlicum, south of S'Hertogenbosch. Their operation was successful, largely due to accurate intelligence from regular patrols. After retiring to Sprang and a period of maintenance and training, the regiment was on the move once again; this time towards Maaseik. The route taken was from Sprang to Loon op Zand, Gheel, Moll, Lille St Hubert, Neerglabbeek, Neeroeteren and finally Maaseik. Having reached Maaseik, the regiment rested and carried out maintenance in readiness for future operations. On 14 November Willy moved with C Squadron to Thorn, under the command of 1/7 Queens Battalion. The official war diaries reported that: 'enemy defensive counter-attack was heavy but no casualties were suffered. Several tanks were bogged down during the advance and the going was extremely bad.'

Meanwhile, back in England, Willy's sister Thea married John Forman on Armistice Day 1944. They were both stationed at Catterick Camp, Yorkshire. He was in the Medical Corps, she in the ATS. John then went off to Egypt and Palestine with the British army. They now have two children, Jim born in 1945 and Jennifer in 1950, five grandchildren and two great-grandchildren. Thea has returned to Germany on numerous occasions for reunions at her old school, but says:

> I can relate well to the present generation, but I do not feel comfortable with Germans of my own generation, especially when they say to me that they knew nothing of what was happening to Jewish families like mine. This I find hard to accept.

Willy was not able to attend the wedding because he was still fighting in Holland. As the 8th Hussars advanced through Holland, they encountered a lot of bombed villages deserted by all but their most elderly residents. Willy recalls:

> The only people left in the villages were the elderly who weren't much use to the Germans. I wish I could have done more for them at the time. In one particular Dutch village we entered, there wasn't a soul around. We drove our tanks to the centre of the village, near the church, and word quickly got around that British troops had arrived. From out of the church, a priest and about twenty children appeared. They had all

been hidden in the basement there. I asked the priest, 'Where is every-body? Where are the Germans?' He replied in Dutch, which I could understand: 'Die Muffe uber der Rhine, nix in der Winkel' – meaning 'The Germans have fled over the Rhine and we've got nothing to eat in the shops.' We had cocoa on our tanks, so I immediately organised all the tanks in our squadron to get out our supplies of cocoa. We gave all the children hot cocoa to drink and chocolate from our compo boxes. Whilst we were relaxing with them, the priest told us that all the men, and even some of the women, of the village had been taken to labour camps by the Germans. How they must have hated the occupying forces and all that Nazism stood for. We were so delighted to have liberated the Dutch people.

Activity by the enemy and the cold weather kept the 8th Hussars and other supporting units busy during the early winter months. On 15 November C Squadron moved with 1/7 Queens Battalion to the area of Ittervoort. The following day they returned to Maaseik where they were given a lecture on the latest situation with the German forces.

The lull in their operations for a couple of days meant that the men could enjoy some relaxation and entertainment: The regiment received complimentary cinema tickets from the Belgian people of Maaseik and the commanding officer was presented with a bouquet of flowers; on 19 November a football team from the 8th Hussars played Maaseik, winning 3–2; and a regimental dance was held in the evening in a local hall. For the rest of November, the men received training in gunnery and learnt about enemy weapons. Maintenance and preparations were under way for the next operation. On 1 and 2 December the regiment moved to Grevenbicht, from where patrols were sent out. The following day, tanks shelled the enemy who were positioned across the Vloed Canal. Patrols were sent out during the night.

On 5 December squadrons came under fire from the enemy. C Squadron moved to Buchten and in the coming days the regiment experienced light attacks from German forces. Between 11 December and Christmas Eve the regiment attended courses and training, with the enemy occasionally probing their defences. Due to operational duties scheduled for C Squadron on Christmas Day, the men celebrated Christmas the day before. On Christmas Day 1944 Willy and his squadron left for Holtum. The war diaries reported: 'Singing heard from enemy lines confirmed that the enemy was celebrating Christmas too.' Willy can confirm hearing singing from the enemy lines that Christmas. Having carried out three days of operational duties, C Squadron returned to Grevenbicht on 27 December. Three days later it took up duties in Gebroek and Buchten. The enemy shelled Gebroek with 88mm guns. C Squadron spent New Year's Eve in Gebroek, with no further enemy activity reported.

New Year's Day 1945 heralded a year that would ultimately see the end of the war. Defeat of Hitler and Nazi forces was still five months away, and Allied troops had yet to invade Germany. On 2 January Willy was with his squadron near Bakenhoven. The war diaries note that at 11 a.m. that day they were subject to enemy sniping. In the next two days the squadron was relieved by B Squadron. The enemy was digging and mining along the front line. On 12 January regimental headquarters moved to Krawinkel. Bakenhoven was finally captured the next day. This was followed by a period of rest and maintenance for the regiment between 13 and 19 January, in readiness for the next operation. It was a hard winter with snow on the ground. Efforts were hampered by thick fog which sometimes reduced visibility to a few hundred yards. The next target was St Joost and, in readiness for the advance on the town, all tanks were whitewashed to serve as camouflage in the snow. Willy remembers it well:

> We had to white-wash our tanks because of the heavy snow on the ground. Moving khaki-coloured vehicles in the snow would have been a prime target for the enemy so all our tanks had to be painted white. It took us a few days to complete.

The camouflaging of tanks was the first stage of Operation Blackcock, designed to bring the Allied front line up to the River Roer. Meanwhile, the Royal Engineers were working flat out constructing bridges and

'Bailey' bridges to enable armoured cars, tanks and other vehicles to cross the numerous streams, rivers and dykes. On 20 January A and C Squadrons were sent out on reconnaissance missions to the region of Hingen and St Joost. The Germans still held St Joost and the vital crossing over the Krom Beek. The task of clearing the town fell to C Squadron and 1 Company 1 Rifle Brigade. The attack began at 2.30 that afternoon. Conditions still had not improved. Amidst thick fog, reduced visibility and snow-covered ground, Willy and his squadron were involved in the intense Battle for St Joost:

> We encountered stiff resistance at St Joost. It was a fierce battle. German paratroops fought every inch of that place. It was a long straggling village which had to be cleared by our forces house by house. Most squadrons of the 8th Hussars were involved. It was here that the men of the Rifle Brigade, fighting alongside us, were kitted out with snow suits and black berets.

Concerning the struggle for St Joost, the war diaries record: 'So exposed was our right that it was possible for the enemy to knock-out two tanks of C Squadron on the road Schilberg–Hingen. Our infantry with close support from C Squadron made some progress in St Joost. But our infantry casualties were heavy in house-to-house fighting.'

The following day came and the battle for the town was still intense. C Squadron lost another tank to a self-propelled gun (SP). Around thirty-four German prisoners were taken. C Squadron was then relieved by B Squadron who, that afternoon, proceeded to knock down house after house with their shells. Flamethrowers were also brought into operation.

On the morning of 24 January, C Squadron gave close-up support to a battalion of 1 Commando Brigade in their attack on Montfort. Bridges had been blown over a nearby stream, making progress difficult. The enemy had withdrawn to the town of Linne, the next Allied target. At 4 p.m. that day, a troop of C Squadron and one troop of Commandos attempted a raid on Linne along the road from de Villa. The infantry and tanks came under heavy fire from SP guns and a suspected MK IV tank in the town. The force commander decided to return to base. The town was still in enemy hands and to take it would require some creative military strategy. This came the following day when a frontal attack on Linne was carried out by 1 Commando Brigade with infantry riding forward on C Squadron tanks under cover of a smoke screen. Willy was involved in the operation:

> Just outside Linne we met with British Commandos and made a Commando charge through the village. We charged our tanks, ten or twelve in a row, towards the village with the Commandos sat on the back. Then they jumped down from our tanks and charged into the main part of the place, clearing the enemy house-by-house where necessary. It took quite a long time to clear the village. It was a tough one, but very exciting at the time. It was the first time that a Commando raid of this kind had taken place so successfully.

The war diaries proudly reported: 'This was the first occasion in which the regiment had worked with commando troops, and the squadron was commended for its co-operation by the Brigadier of 1 Commando Brigade.' German forces began to withdraw overnight, retreating over the River Roer thus enabling 3 Commando and C Squadron to secure the town, although the wood south-east of Linne was heavily mined, being hazardous for advancing troops. Willy's squadron then retired for a week of maintenance and rest. Lieutenant-Colonel G.R.D. Fitzpatrick MBE, MC took command of the regiment. During this time, the commanding officer outlined future operations. In the January 1945 edition of *The Illustrated London News*, a report was published about the final clearing of the Roer Triangle:

> The capture of Linne by a famous Commando (which previously led the invasion into Sicily and Italy) – riding on tanks of an armoured division charging across the snow-bound plain and crashing right into the village and hurling out the defenders – a most spectacular and successful action completely surprising the enemy and crushing the last strong point between Maas and Roer.

During the whole campaign, the 8th Hussars were accompanied by Brian de Grinean, a reporter and illustrator for *The Illustrated London News*, who sketched in detail both battles of St Joost and Linne, as well as the liberation of Fallingbostel Allied POW camp. Copies of his drawings were later given to Willy, which he has kept to this day.

The regimental history summarised the accomplishment of Operation Blackcock on Linne and St Joost as twofold: 'first, for the successful deployment of an Armoured Division in mid-winter over snow, and secondly, as the first occasion that the Division had ever operated with Commando troops.'

At 9.30 a.m. on 2 February 1945, the regiment began its move to Koningsbosch. The route took the tanks through Schilberg and Echterbosch to Koningsbosch. B Squadron of the 8th Hussars was sent to Waldfeucht, with one troop detachment in Bruggelchen. It was the first squadron of the 8th Hussars to enter Germany. Meanwhile, the rest of the division remained in its positions overlooking the River Maas, waiting for orders to cross. Willy's squadron remained in the Netherlands for the time being on training exercises. The entry in the war diary for 5 February comments on conditions for the regiment: 'all roads were disintegrating rapidly owing to a very heavy thaw and movement was becoming so difficult that it was doubtful if the regiment could have operated if called upon to do so.' The following day orders were received for it to move. At 8.30 a.m. on 7 February it set off for Grevenbicht, via Koningsbosch, Schilberg, Susteren and Roosteren. For tank drivers it was a difficult time, as Willy says:

> We were hampered by the thaw which meant that our tanks were sometimes bogged down. We had to be towed about three miles out of Koningsbosch, conditions were so bad. In Grevenbicht we carried out further maintenance on our tanks. We also had courses in gunnery and wireless.

On 11 February the regiment was inspected by Major General L.O. Lyne of the 7th Armoured Division. He gave a detailed lecture to all officers and NCOs about the important part that the regiment had played in clearing the enemy out of the Roer-Maas Triangle. He also complimented C Squadron on its part in the fighting in Linne and St Joost the previous month.

The tanks now had to be prepared for entry into Germany in conditions with no snowfall. The whitened tanks had to be repainted with a new coat of khaki camouflage paint. This was carried out over several days from 12–16 February. From 17–18 February, all men received firing practice on the ranges. Then the regiment moved back to Maaseik. While they were there, members of C Squadron gave a demonstration of firing on ranges which was watched by the general officer-in-command of 7th Armoured Division and representatives from all units in the brigade.

Much of February and early March 1945 was spent in maintenance and training ahead of the crossing of the Rhine. Re-equipment and extensive training of all fighting units was essential to the success of the next major offensive – the invasion of Germany, codenamed Operation Plunder. On 5 March the regiment prepared to move from Maaseik to an area south of Zomeren. On arrival, the regiment was billeted along the line of the canal south of Zomeren. In the afternoon of 7 March, tanks of C Squadron carried out firing practice on the shooting ranges. Subsequent days were spent on collective training, including demonstration of the use of a bulldozer to clear road blocks and mine testing.

During their free time, the men played football matches or were engaged in other recreational exercise. Between 18 and 22 March they carried out further firing practice on the ranges ready for the occupation of Germany. St Patrick's Day fell during this period:

We were stationed near several canals at this time. That St Patrick's Day of 1945, we were each issued with a Shamrock for the morning parade, which we wore with pride. It was also a custom for that one day for sergeants and officers to serve other ranks in the Mess. During the day we had masses of fun constructing makeshift boats out of wooden boxes. We then had mock fights on the nearby canal, during which most of us fell in the water. We also drank a lot and had football matches. We had a wonderful time which was very important for us because the stress and tension of recent fighting had to be relieved. After all, we had been through so much since we landed in June the previous year.

On 24 March the 8th Hussars were given orders to prepare to move to Geldern. The huge task of packing up began. The men had been in the same location for several weeks. The war diaries note that day: 'A grand view of the airborne operations was witnessed, the entire party flying over our location continuously for four hours.' Willy also remembers the event:

> This was the real excitement now. Masses of airborne forces passed overhead. It was awesome and historic for us. We were witnessing history in front of our very eyes. They were flying ahead of us to prepare the way for our advance into Germany. We had known all along, ever since D-Day, that our final destination would be the invasion of Germany. It was what I had joined the Royal Armoured Corps for – to be part of the taking of Germany back from Nazi tyranny, the brutality of which I had personally experienced myself in Bonn and Dachau.

At 2 p.m. the following day, 25 March, Willy moved with his regiment near Geldern. They crossed a Bailey bridge constructed by the Royal Engineers at Needeweert. Congestion on the bridge was heavy due to the volume of vehicles forming up as part of the invasion force. The regiment reached Geldern at 5 p.m. The next day the commanding officer briefed all ranks about the forthcoming crossing of the Rhine. At first light, Major Huth, second-in-command of the regiment, had moved off with reconnaissance parties to a harbour north of the Rhine. The rest of the men waited with anticipation. 'We waited patiently,' says Willy, 'whilst the Royal Engineers tried to finish the Bailey bridge for us to cross. Meanwhile there was a lot of aerial bombardment and shelling of our positions by the enemy, but somehow our squadron managed to escape any damage.'

Then orders were received for the crossing of the Rhine to take place the following day. The 8th Hussars, at the head of 131 Infantry Brigade, began its move to a road north of Geldern. For Willy it was a strange time:

None of us knew how severe the fighting in Germany would be. For me it was strange in a way because I had not set foot on German soil for six years and so much had happened to me in that time. I had no idea how I would feel and neither did I have a clue about my family I had left behind in Bonn.

CHAPTER 8

THE INVASION OF GERMANY

Tuesday 27 March 1945 dawned on what would be a momentous day for Willy. His regiment had been told that this would be the day they would cross the Rhine into Germany. The crossing was due to take place in darkness and at three main points for Allied forces: at Rees, Xanten and Wesel. They would be covered by airborne landings that would seize the bridges intact. The 8th Hussars began moving at 9.30 a.m. along minor roads. They had only progressed half a mile when all further roads were blocked by Allied traffic. Willy's squadron was diverted to the main highway from Geldern to Venlo. When they reached the highway, the war diaries record that they were met with 'a line of traffic nose-to-croup and it was impossible to even get onto the main road'. They were forced to linger for several hours. Willy recalls:

It was badly congested on the roads, but that was to be expected given the sheer volume of vehicles heading towards the Rhine. There didn't appear to be any traffic control in place ahead of us but we felt confident that everything was going according to plan. We had faith in our military leaders. While we waited to cross we saw and heard artillery bombs continuously falling but somehow we were lucky. We never got hit. It wasn't until dark that we could finally make progress on our route.

At eleven o'clock that night, C Squadron led the regiment over the Rhine, crossing at Xanten in brilliant moonlight. They were finally on German soil. Movement of vehicles was slow on the other side due to congestion on the narrow secondary roads. C Squadron spent the night not far from the banks of the Rhine. How did it feel to be in Germany? Willy's response is honest and humbling:

I always wanted to get on with the fighting and be back on German soil to defeat the Nazis. In reality, that was our sole aim. It was euphoric for me when we crossed the Rhine and were finally in Germany. I had looked forward to this victorious moment for so long. I was never scared, but it was tinged with sadness and regret that my original tank crew did not live to see this day. They were left behind, buried in an Allied war cemetery and that was tough for me. We lived with the daily reality that we might be killed or lose our comrades – that is the nature of war, but it doesn't shelter one from the pain of losing one's closest mates in battle. I had to carry on with a new crew – and that took some adjustment. We had a job to do – we had to carry on.

Now that we had entered Germany, we were *taking* not liberating. We liberated Ghent, liberated Eindhoven, etc., but we *took* Germany, *took* Hamburg. France, Belgium and Holland were all occupied by the Germans and we had to liberate them before we could get to Germany. I felt sorry for the French, the Belgians and the Dutch but never for the German people. We witnessed utter devastation and the total defeat of Germany, but not once did I feel pity for them. Although we did not yet know the full extent of the Holocaust, I knew what the Germans were capable of, having been four months in Dachau myself. It was my duty to make sure that Germany was absolutely defeated. But, it was not my place to exact revenge on the Germans I encountered. I talked to POWs, interrogated them but I always behaved with the utmost decency because I knew how I was treated in Dachau and I should not behave like the Nazis. That would have been wrong. I never took anything from

German soldiers (like watches or belongings). My aim was to get rid of Adolf Hitler, but not to kill people unnecessarily, no matter what had been done to me.

On 28 March the regiment received orders to move to Brunen under the command of Major Huth. En route to Brunen Willy's squadron passed through Dursfordter Wald and Hamminkeln. The entry in the war diaries for that day notes that the regiment 'passed through the main dropping and landing zones of the operation carried out by 6th Airborne Division. Many crash gliders were seen and it was clear that the operation, though successful, had been expensive.' Orders were received to advance to Raesfeld. Willy's squadron led the advance and arrived in Raesfeld at about two o'clock that afternoon. The town had already been cleared by 22nd Armoured Brigade Group. Then C Squadron spread out to the north and east of Raesfeld, with a patrol sent south to link up with the 6th Airborne Division. Occasional shelling by German guns caused one casualty. The war diaries comment: 'except for a few odd shells at about 0400 hours, the regiment had a quiet night.'

The ultimate destination for the 8th Hussars was Hamburg. Between the Rhine and Hamburg there were a number of key river crossings which presented significant obstacles to the invading forces: the Rhine itself; the Dortmund-Ems Canal; the Weser-Ems Canal; and the rivers Weser, Aller and Elbe. On 29 March the regiment advanced to the southern outskirts of Borken which had the previous day been reached by the 5th Royal Tanks and was already occupied by the 5th Dragoon Guards and the 9th Durham Light Infantry. They had encountered stiff resistance from the enemy. That morning, C Squadron was ordered to the north to carry out flank protection of the Borken–Weseke road. Heavy rain in recent days hampered the move – tanks became bogged down in the soft, sandy soil. The Royal Engineers worked tirelessly to improve the conditions of the roads. The 8th Hussars also experienced sporadic attack from a few enemy SP guns. C Squadron was then ordered to move to Borkenwirth and occupy the main road from Borken to Burlo. Enemy guns could be heard firing to the south. C Squadron met some opposition while going over a railway crossing but this was dealt with successfully.

According to the regiment's war diaries, on 30 March they headed north along the Gr. Burlo–Öding road. They came under mortar fire and sniping to the north. The leading troop was attacked in a wooded area by Germans armed with bazookas and two tanks were quickly withdrawn. It became clear that it would be impossible to use the road through the woods without clearing the area with infantry supported by tanks. The war diary entry for that day is very detailed:

> The woods were thick and came right down to the road. The leading troop of A Squadron was virtually written-off. Lt Anstey was killed. Two tanks managed to advance to the stream on the southern outskirts of Öding. One had been knocked out, the other forced to withdraw when its commander Sgt Constable was badly wounded in the head. The woods were successfully cleared by 1 Coy of 1 Royal Brigade … Vehicles got stuck in mud. Sgt Taylor of B Squadron captured fifty German paratroopers, the enemy was forced to withdraw.

Some Germans escaped to the east where they were firmly entrenched. These men were part of Battle Group Primus, a party of die-hard Nazis from Hermann Goering's troops of the 7th Parachute Division. Willy comments that: 'these German soldiers fought with great determination. They were not prepared to surrender. They had made a pact to fight to the bitter end. And that surprised us in a way because they had no chance against the sheer mass of Allied forces now advancing through their country – and that included American and Canadian troops.'

Regimental headquarters and C Squadron harboured in the area of Burlo. There had been heavy losses: A Squadron had lost four tanks, with another badly damaged; Lt Anstey had been killed, six other ranks killed and three other ranks injured. Six were reported missing, believed to have been taken prisoner. B Squadron reported four men wounded in action. The regiment had taken 106 enemy soldiers prisoner and killed around fifty in the intense fighting. The reality of war was all around them, as Willy describes:

We were outside somewhere trying to be relieved by the Guards Armoured Division and for some reason, they didn't come. I was sitting in my tank and all of a sudden Moaning Minnies landed all around us. These were bombs which shattered all over the place and were really quite lethal. One of my friends was on another tank and was hit. He was lying on the ground badly injured. I got out of my tank to tend to him. He was injured in the leg and foot. I bandaged his leg, put something around his foot and another officer came along to help. Together we lifted him onto a stretcher and carried him over ploughed fields for at least a mile to the nearest first-aid station. The officer was 6'2" and I was only 5'6" or 5'8". I was carrying the back of the stretcher, he the front. It was such hard work because of his height. The Moaning Minnies were still dropping everywhere around us, but luckily none of them hit us. We finally got to the first-aid station, handed him over to the medical officer and made our way back to the tanks as quickly as possible. For this action, the officer was Mentioned in Despatches. Never mind me! I was only a trooper! I found out later on that our wounded comrade recovered and that it was thanks to me bandaging his foot that it was saved from being amputated.

At first light on 31 March the regiment moved up to Öding and with 131 Brigade were given the task of clearing the town. Just after five o'clock that day, C Squadron led the rest of the regiment to block roads to the north on the Vreden to Ottenstein route. The war diary records: 'a quiet night was spent with no action by the enemy on any part of the front.' Earlier that day, an interesting German military figure had surrendered to the regiment. The war diary devotes a full typed page to his capture:

On the 'I' [intelligence] side the most interesting prisoner was Oberst Primus, Commander of the German 4 Para Ers. Regiment. This nice clueless old body clocked in on our Forward Squadron after being out of touch with higher formations for two days. His last order was to report to Winterswijk but bearing in mind the reception given to stragglers by 2 Para Army's Field Court Martials he sent his Adjutant and dossed down. He willingly elucidated the picture so far as he knew it ... Oberst Primus is a handsome and dignified, if slightly vague, old buffer. His regiment, which he insisted was a Training regiment and not intended for active service, was brought down from Holland and put under the command of 15 PG Division. On 29 March he was ordered to hold sector Rhede–Burlo. On his right were troops of 7 Para Division. Later during the same day, our tanks broke through on his left, and he asked 15 PG Division for permission to withdraw. This was refused. By the time the situation had become really chaotic, Division rang up again granting permission to withdraw in the direction of Winterswijk and ordering Primus to report to a Command Post at Lammers, south of Winterswijk. He was just about to set off for the Command Post when he realised that this was probably an invitation to be shot by a Mobile Court Martial; so he told his Adjutant to go instead and walked over to the nearest British troops.

The lengthy report gives an important insight into the disintegration that was beginning to permeate the German forces, even among its highest ranks who were no longer prepared to risk their lives for Hitler. This was borne out by the official regimental history of the 7th Royal Armoured Division which said:

> ... as we advanced farther and faster, the enemy's disorganisation was to become increasingly apparent, since German units tended to have less and less conception as to its general position. The supply system, except behind the parachutists on our left, was disintegrating equally with the chain of command.

On the morning of 1 April, the 8th Hussars moved through Ahaus, Heek and Metelen en route for Wettringen. They parked just outside Rheine, four miles south-west of Wettringen. For the next two days the regiment waited for infantry to clear areas held by thousands of enemy troops. In the meantime, patrols were sent out to gather intelligence on enemy positions. German opposition continued to be strong in the region of Ibbenburen. From 4 April, the 8th Hussars fought alongside the

22nd Armoured Brigade and 11th Armoured Division. At seven o'clock that evening C Squadron and one company of 1/5 Queens led a composite advance guard under the command of Major Firth. Willy was tank driver for Major Firth and was the lead tank.

The roads were heavily congested with military traffic and progress was slow. At 10.30 p.m. they reached the bridge over the railway at Langenbeck, which Willy remembers:

It was here that we experienced attacks by German infantry and bazooka fire which held up our advance. We also sustained another casualty when Lt Pim's tank was hit and he was severely wounded. His driver and gunner continued and drove their tank over the bridge, disappearing into the distance beyond us. The infantry [of 1/5 Queens] started to clear the houses on the south side of the railway. When they had completed the task, one of their platoons was sent north to make contact with Lt Pim's tank. They were attacked by the enemy and suffered seven casualties. The situation became confused and further action was called off.

The official war diaries concluded the following: 'This was not a satisfactory operation and it is considered that night advance against unreconnoitred positions, on a narrow front, are not a practical op of war.'

At first light the following day, 5 April, Willy's squadron under command of 1/5 Queens successfully cleared the remainder of the houses north of Langenbeck. By midday they were concentrated at Halem. The advance continued on 6 April through Engter to Gr. Lessen. The following day the regiment pushed towards Vilsen. Although over a hundred German POWs were taken, and six 20mm AA guns seized, A Squadron lost one tank. The war diary for 7 April reported:

Opposition in Vilsen. Plans were being made to attack and clear the village. Citizens telephoned to houses on the crossroads to say they were anxious to surrender. C Squadron was ordered to move into the area immediately. One Coy, 1/5 Queens proceeded to clear the village. By 1200 hours this was achieved. Regiment 8th group ordered to capture intact the bridge over the Weser.

C Squadron was ordered to advance on the route from Vilsen to Susdedt via Godestorf, Eminghausen and Thedinghausen. They encountered stiff opposition at Godestorf and more on the southern edge of Eminghausen. Willy recalls:

> We were held up by bazooka fire. Our Lt Jephson was wounded and two of our tanks were knocked out. We successfully cleared Eminghausen by nightfall and moved off to Thedinghausen. We encountered further opposition during our advance and we received orders to stop for the night. To our surprise, we cleared Thedinghausen the following day with little difficulty.

That day, 8 April, C Squadron lost another tank during its advance north-east when one of four self-propelled guns in the region of Holtorflunsen knocked it out. Meanwhile, B Squadron tried to silence SP guns near the bridge across the canal east of Eissel. At about 1500 hours the SP guns were withdrawn north and the bridge was blown. A, B and C Squadrons were ordered to move on the town of Riede from different angles. The war diaries commented: 'C Squadron fired a large number of rounds into the town which was soon in flames.' The town was success-fully cleared by nightfall.

> As we advanced through Germany, most of the houses we were billeted in were empty. German civilians had fled. I used to meet some Germans who were in terrible disarray. They realised the Führer's vision had come to an end, the war was going to be over and they would be totally defeated. I noticed also that with the prisoners who surrendered to us so easily, all wanted the war to finish. There were still die-hard fighters who denied they were going to lose and continued fighting to the bitter end, but the majority of ordinary Germans could see the war was drawing to a close.

All squadrons were engaged in fighting on a daily basis. The advance towards Sudweyhe continued at first light on 9 April. En route a large number of enemy were killed, and an equally significant number cap-tured, although precise numbers are not recorded in the war diary.

C Squadron was ordered to pass through Sudweyhe whilst the other squadrons mopped up in the town. Willy headed with his squadron for Leeste and Brinkum. At one of the crossroads they met stiff opposition from the same SS troop that had caused them problems in Kirchweyhe and Sudweyhe. It was established that these German troops belonged to the 12 SS Ers Bn, and consisted of somewhere between 300 and 500 men. A reconnaissance troop was sent north to observe enemy troop movements north of Brinkum. It was deemed necessary to call in air support, which the 8th Hussars received from the RAF. Later it was learned that the bomber pilots had had the best target of German positions for days.

Just before last light, a company of 1/5 Queens finally entered Leeste and engaged the enemy. Meanwhile, C Squadron waited at a crossroads outside the town for orders to move in. A German anti-tank gun suddenly appeared and penetrated one of C Squadron's tanks. The gun was knocked out but it became clear that C Squadron could not take Leeste and Brinkum without considerable infantry support. That would have to wait until the following day. Further injury was inflicted by the enemy on 10 April, as Willy comments:

> Leeste and Brinkum were stubbornly held by German forces. Although we had achieved so much in a relatively short space of time, and fighting was sometimes sporadic, it was still dangerous for us. When we patrolled forward of the front line and engaged with the enemy in Leeste, another of our tanks in C Squadron was blown up by a mine and the gunner killed. Another tank became bogged down in the mud and came under fire. The crew had to abandon the tank.

On 11 April C Squadron moved south with the regiment to an area near Nienburg. It was here that they carried out vital maintenance and had opportunity to rest. 'We were really tired from the fighting,' says Willy, 'and our fairly rapid advance through Germany. It is not really ever possible to relax when you are advancing towards enemy positions. One is always vulnerable.' The men remained in the area another day, receiving their first bath for weeks, with an opportunity to go to the cinema in the afternoon. Now they were preparing for the crossing of the River Weser.

At 9.30 a.m. on 13 April, the 8th Hussars began their crossing of the Weser at Nienburg and proceeded to an area north, ready to form a bridgehead over the River Aller at Rethem. Having crossed the Weser, they spent time in maintenance and rest. Crossing the Aller was delayed because 53 Division had difficulty establishing a bridgehead over the river. During 14 April, the Royal Engineers constructed a class 40 floating Bailey bridge over the Aller to enable troops to cross the next day. As it happened, Willy and his squadron rolled their tanks over a bridge further south, heading for Duishorn. Routes were heavily blocked and they were unable to get through. They themselves suffered no attack from German forces, but other squadrons of the 8th Hussars were not so lucky. They encountered enemy opposition immediately after crossing the Aller.

On 16 April, B and C Squadrons were given the order to advance on Fallingbostel, passing through Duishorn. A Squadron was directed to cross the River Bohme by bridge and establish itself north of Fallingbostel. It was suspected that a large camp holding Allied POWs was located in woods south-west of the town of Fallingbostel. If so, it would be the task of Willy's squadron to liberate it. Reconnaissance troops were sent out to locate the camp. They returned with information about the existence of a large Allied POW camp, also containing displaced persons. It was Stalag 11B holding 6,500 British and American prisoners, and Stalag 357 with some 3,500 POWs. Some of the Allied prisoners had been there for nearly a year since the operation in the difficult region of Villers-Bocage in France. Willy was involved in its liberation:

> We were driving down a tree-lined road and suddenly the camp was visible on our left. It consisted mainly of low huts, surrounded by barbed wire with a wooden watchtower at the entrance. By now, they must have seen us coming because all the inmates were climbing onto the roofs of the huts and were cheering and waving to us. We liberated Fallingbostel camp, but then our squadron was ordered to move on with the fighting. It fell to B Squadron to enter the camp. I do remember that as we drove our tanks past the camp, we received a tremendous welcome from the POWs. The liberation of the camp was reported in the newspapers back in Britain, and to have been part of that gave us a sense of achievement.

The report in the official war diaries for the 8th Hussars noted of Fallingbostel POW camp: 'On the whole the prisoners appeared to be in good order and gave our patrols a most tumultuous welcome.'

The next operation involved the town of Fallingbostel itself and required considerable firepower and riflemen to overpower the enemy in the streets and houses. The infantry had to clear the place house by house. C Squadron was ordered to find an intact bridge to cross the River Bohme to the north-east of Fallingbostel. By mid-afternoon they had reached the southern outskirts of Dorfmark.

> As we advanced at this time, all the bridges in the area had been blown by the enemy. It meant that the Royal Engineers had their work cut out constructing bridges for us to cross the rivers.

A plan was hatched to clear Dorfmark of enemy positions. The autobahn had not been completed, making it all but impassable to the regiment except for tracked vehicles. A reconnaissance troop was sent out to find an alternative route across country. On 17 April the regiment's squadrons joined up from their locations and advanced together on the route from Dorfmark to Kroge, Bommelsen and into Frielinger. Casualties and damage to tanks were suffered by A and B Squadrons. C Squadron advanced towards Heber, encountering slight enemy resistance, and then continued towards Hillern.

While the 8th Hussars had been engaged on operations around Fallingbostel, British forces had liberated Belsen concentration camp on 15 April. Nothing could prepare the liberators for the utter horror of what they saw. Piles of thousands of rotting emaciated corpses lay in hastily dug open pits. Those who had survived were in a terrible condition; thousands would die in the coming days from starvation and disease. British troops, medical staff and Jewish chaplains undertook to tend to the immediate needs of the survivors. Willy's squadron passed Belsen concentration camp at this time:

> We were very near the concentration camp, but my commanding officer said to me: 'I don't want you to go in there, Willy'. He had extraordinary

compassion and understanding. By now we knew of some of the atrocities against the Jews and, because I am Jewish, he did not want me to experience the horror. I still did not know at this point about my family. I began to fear that they might have suffered the same fate or that they were even in Belsen.

At first light on 18 April, Willy's squadron moved with the regiment towards Welle where they encountered stiff resistance in the forest of Langeloh. Any progress was impossible without considerable force at their disposal. A route that bypassed the forest was devised. The next problem was to cross the railway to reach Tostedt. C Squadron was ordered through Otter and towards high ground beyond. The railway bridge was undefended but the approaches were impassable. C Squadron found another route over the railway for the whole regiment. After two of its tanks had crossed the bridge, it collapsed and Willy's squadron spent time reconstructing it. They then established themselves to the right of the bridge and set about clearing Wistedt. The leading troop of C Squadron encountered opposition from snipers and bazookas but by early evening C Squadron had established itself in Wistedt.

The following day, 19 April, the 8th Hussars moved on Dohren and then to the southern outskirts of Hollenstedt. They met enemy resistance en route and one tank was wrecked. Patrols were sent to Oldendorf, Wennerstorf and Wenzendorf to gather intelligence on enemy positions. At Oldendorf the patrol captured a number of Hamburg policemen who had been sent out to protect the autobahn. In the region of Wenzendorf, the patrol liberated a Russian POW camp and inspected a local aerodrome. It fell to C Squadron with 1/5 Queens to clear and consolidate Hollenstedt. As they advanced through Germany, the disintegration of the defeated country was evident. Willy comments:

When we arrived in various villages and outlying areas, most of the farms were deserted. Everyone appeared to have left, or at least the fit able men and women. It was always our duty to go right through the barns to check for booby-traps, etc. We had to be very careful because sometimes German troops set up traps to ordinary items that we might take, like binoculars which seemed innocent, but if picked up would set off a trap. This trick was well known and we were constantly warned about it in training sessions. Very often we came across basements in the farmhouses where the farmers had stocked a lot of food which was well-preserved in glass bottles. These were mainly vegetables which we were able to use ourselves to add to our rations. The villages were more often than not very quiet and we never found out where the inhabitants had gone. The only people we came across sometimes were the elderly. I was always able to talk to them in German to gather information which was quite useful to our regiment. Very often they were too frightened to talk, saying 'we don't know anything'.

On 20 April Willy's squadron was ordered into Schwiederstorf and was instructed to patrol towards the village of Daerstorf and capture it. The lead troop of C Squadron came under fire from the west of Daerstorf and one tank was damaged. An SP gun was seen in the vicinity. In the early morning mist, one carrier patrol had worked round to within 500 yards east of Daerstorf and knocked out a tracked gun-tower. The enemy was well-ensconced in the village so it was decided that, under cover of smoke, one troop of C Squadron under Lt Gould would move across the open countryside and attack the village from the east. During the action, Lt Gould slightly lost direction and attacked from the south-east, but fortunately was able to overrun and destroy an anti-tank detachment. He was wounded in the head, but carried on with his troop until ordered out of action later. The war diaries reported on the clearing of Daerstorf: 'Once in the village, which was now blazing fiercely, considerable enemy opposition was encountered.' By now, the rest of the regiment was attacking from the south and north-east and were subjected to very heavy shellfire. At three o'clock that afternoon, Daerstof was successfully captured. The war diaries concluded:

It contained no less than three anti-tank guns and 200 infantry. Some of the enemy escaped north, but B Squadron killed and captured a number of Germans. C Squadron proceeded with Coy, 1 Rifle Brigade to clear Wulmstorf. Patrols were sent out to the high ground overlooking the river

Elbe. It turned out to be the last serious action of the war and it entailed comparatively small loss.

The war was heading towards its closing stages. The next stage of operations was crossing the River Elbe, west of Hamburg. The city of Hamburg was the ultimate destination for troops, including the 8th Hussars. The entry in the war diary for 21 April reads: 'The task of the 7th Armoured Division was now the consolidation of the boundary reached, the high ground overlooking the Elbe, pending putting into effect the plans for the capture of Hamburg.' They were supported by 131 Brigade and the 22nd Armoured Brigade. The left flank of the division was protected by the 11th Hussars. At this time C Squadron was in Daerstorf in support of 1/5 Queens Infantry.

Willy's squadron was still in Daerstorf on 22 April when a German ammunition train arrived from the west. It was quickly engaged by the squadron and one of its trucks burst into flames. The driver unhooked his engine and disappeared in the direction of Hamburg. C Squadron proceeded to destroy the remaining trucks. An hour later the engine driver, who had obviously received different orders, reappeared to salvage the train. The engine was dealt with by a few shots from British tanks, which blew up when a shot hit its boiler. During that day, twenty POWs were captured, having surrendered themselves.

At last light four enemy aircraft attacked Elstorf, dropping four bombs, two of which fell within 50 yards of the office of regimental headquarters but no damage was done. By 23 April, C Squadron was relieved by A Squadron and withdrew to Scheiderstorf where it remained until the end of the month. On 29 April C Squadron moved back to Daerstorf. It had been a month in which the squadron had suffered fourteen casualties and two fatalities. That same day, the 6th Airborne Division with the 11th Armoured Division had reached Wismar and Lübeck on the Baltic. German forces in Czechoslovakia and Bavaria were disintegrating. Italy surrendered to Field Marshal Alexander. Willy comments:

By now it was clear that the war was drawing to a close. We heard that the Russians had broken the Berlin front and the Americans had crossed the Elbe. The capture of Hamburg was the last obstacle facing the 8th Hussars.

On 30 April 1945 Adolf Hitler and his newly-wed mistress Eva Braun committed suicide in his underground bunker in Berlin. In taking his own life, Hitler ensured that the Allied powers could not bring him to justice. In the coming months, extensive investigations were carried out by British and American intelligence officers to verify his death. For Willy and his comrades, news of Hitler's death did not reach them until they arrived in Hamburg nearly a week later:

> We were constantly on the move, mopping up operations en route to Hamburg. We were isolated from news of world events and that, surprising as it may seem, included news of the death of Hitler. We had no newspapers or broadcasts. We were getting on with the job in hand. We were nearing the end of the war and were kept busy with our squadrons. The main fighting as far as we are concerned was almost finished.

CHAPTER 9

THE CAPTURE OF HAMBURG AND END OF THE WAR

By early May 1945, much of the fighting was over. German forces were disintegrating and surrendering to Allied powers. The 8th Hussars were preparing for the final stage of operations – the capture of Hamburg. Reconnaissance patrols were regularly sent out from all squadrons to look for a suitable route to advance south of Hamburg. The military strategists had identified two important goals in the capture of Hamburg: first, the seizure of intact bridges over the Elbe and second, the safeguarding of Hamburg Docks. On the evening of 3 May the regiment moved to Marmstorf just as it was getting dark. It secured the high ground and stayed there the night with a view to advancing at 5.15 a.m. the next day. Willy recalls an encounter at this time with a young German soldier:

On our way to Hamburg we stopped for a while at the roadside. I heard crying in the distance and got out of my tank. It was coming from bushes ahead. Then I spotted a young German soldier. He looked no more than fifteen or sixteen years old. He begged me in German: 'Don't shoot me, don't shoot me. I surrender.' I replied in German, to which he was very surprised. I told him: 'Don't worry about it. You're safe.' He was still deeply upset and said: 'Yes, my commanding officer told me that if I am captured,

I would be shot.' I reassured him again that everything would be okay for him. I even gave him a cigarette.

The following day, 4 May, the regiment advanced on Hamburg. Their brief was to guard the main approaches north and west of the city. The war diaries reported that: 'The march through the town was uneventful.' By 7.30 that morning the 8th Hussars were holding the city, with C Squadron guarding all approaches from the west. Willy comments:

> I took part in the capture of Hamburg. It was an exciting time for us. Luckily the bridges were still intact and we were able to proceed slowly into the city itself. Behind us a huge volume of armoured vehicles was following. It was an amazing experience. We didn't suffer any losses because by this time there was little resistance. The Germans were in disarray. The city had been completely destroyed. The RAF raids had inflicted heavy bombing on Hamburg. Many parts of the dock area were completely flattened. I was busy interrogating POWs who had marched towards us in their thousands to surrender. North of Hamburg, the Wehrmacht [German army] was surrendering in huge numbers to Allied forces. Over the next few days, until VE Day [8 May 1945], we had the task of disarming the Wehrmacht. We were billeted in a beautiful house outside Hamburg and German prisoners arrived in their thousands. It was quite something to witness the total defeat of the Nazis. My commanding officer Captain Firth asked me to deal with the prisoners. I was involved in interrogating them and carried out various translation work. I also organised them into working parties to do shift work in the officers' mess and canteens.

At three o'clock on 4 May, B Squadron stopped a German staff car which had arrived at Quickborn with a message from Admiral Doenitz; the admiral was prepared to talk about the surrender of the German armies facing the 21 Army Group. An hour later, the commander-in chief of the German Army North arrived and set off with General Dempsey for the centre of Hamburg. Events were moving at a rapid pace. The war diaries for the 8th Hussars recorded that: 'At 2100hrs news of the capitulation of all the German forces in north-west Europe was heard over the BBC news. This was followed by a British War report broadcast over the Hamburg radio.' The person who gave the first Allied propaganda broadcast in German on Radio Hamburg to the German people was none other than Willy's ex-German Jewish friend from 248 Pioneer Company, Geoffrey Perry (Horst Pinschewer). His story is told in detail in his autobiography *When Life Becomes History*.

While Willy was in Hamburg, his squadron parked their tanks outside the Rathaus (Town Hall). It was to lead to an unexpected find, as Willy explains:

> There we were with our tanks lined up outside the famous Rathaus. Next to the Rathaus was a large heavy door. We wondered what was behind there. We drove our tank straight for the door which revealed a long dark cellar. Right at the end we found an enormous store of German champagne hidden. We discovered that the cellar and its contents belonged to von Ribbentrop [Foreign Secretary under Hitler]. We used some for ourselves and then reported its finding to our Commanding Officer. We were able to celebrate the end of the war with that champagne! In 1998, when my wife Judy and I visited Hamburg for a long weekend, I showed her where I had driven my tank and parked it outside the Rathaus. Of course for me it was an emotional time – Hamburg was now such a wonderful, peaceful place. The last time I had seen it was in such different circumstances and bomb-damaged. I went up to the policeman on guard outside the Rathaus and said: 'Do you know, this is where I stood with my tank in 1945 after we captured Hamburg.' He thought it was incredible for me to be returning to the same spot.

On 5 May 1945 the regiment was on the move, but its locations are all encoded in the war diary. By 6 May an order was received that a move to the region of the Kiel Canal was imminent. The following day, the regiment was on an hour's notice to move. At 11.00 a.m. the commanding officer went to brigade headquarters and was told the news that Germany was signing a treaty of unconditional surrender which would come into effect at one minute past midnight on 8 May. The

8th Hussars began their move through Hasloh to Pinneberg, then north to Elmshorn, further north to Itzehoe and finally to Wacken, west of Neumünster, where regimental headquarters set itself up in a farmhouse. The BBC announced that the next day, 8 May, would be VE day. Willy's squadron remained in Itzehoe. 'We listened with relief,' says Willy, 'that the war was officially over in Europe. Of course, on the ground we knew the reality that Germany was defeated.'

May 8th 1945 dawned on what would forever be commemorated as VE Day – Victory in Europe. The men of the 8th Hussars spent that morning carrying out maintenance on the tanks and vehicles. At three o'clock that afternoon they listened to Prime Minister Winston Churchill's broadcast from London. Willy remembers listening to Churchill's speech on radios in Itzehoe where they were stationed. It was a stirring speech, in which the man who had led Britain from May 1940 throughout the war to victory, told the people:

This is your victory! It is the victory of the cause of freedom in every land. In all our long history we have never seen a greater day than this. Everyone, man or woman, has done their best. Neither the long years, nor the dangers, nor the fierce attacks of the enemy, have in any way weakened the independent resolve of the British nation.

Listening to that speech with his squadron, Willy himself knew the price of losing one's freedom. Churchill's triumphant words resounded through him, and as he wandered through the streets in the coming days, he could feel justly proud that he had done his bit for the defeat of Hitler. Now, the Nazi regime lay as rubble at his feet, totally defeated. Later that day, his regiment hoisted the Union Jack flag in Hamburg, a symbol that British troops now occupied the city. The war diaries recorded: 'The regiment had been issued with a Union Jack and this was flown from the top of the biggest wireless aerial that could be erected.' At nine o'clock that evening, they heard King George VI's broadcast to the Empire. It was a day to remember. 'We celebrated a lot that day,' recalls Willy. 'There was plenty of beer and we got drunk! We were happy that the war was over.' While Willy was stationed in Itzehoe, various football matches were organised against other regiments. He found himself playing against his good friend Gerry Moore in the 22nd Armoured Brigade. They shook hands and secretly made a pact not to tackle each other.

On 9 May, the 8th Hussars moved further north still to the area of Friedrichstadt. Willy's squadron was posted at a check-point at the level-crossing to disarm trains and direct stragglers to reception areas. The overall role of the 8th Hussars was to marshal, disarm and organise the movement of German military personnel into the Schleswig-Holstein Peninsula. Willy's squadron settled into the work of disarming German military forces in the region. Patrols were sent to outlying areas. They discovered an ammunition dump near Wesselburen which was promptly destroyed. Four German soldiers were captured trying to cross the River Eider by ferry. One troop of C Squadron was sent with a platoon of 2 Devons to visit the villages of Midstedt, Rantrum, Oldensbeck, Winnert and Hollingstedt. They were to disarm German troops and arrest any SS men that they came across. They returned that evening having destroyed approximately 2,500 enemy rifles and machine guns. The following day similar duties were carried out, searching for any supplies of enemy ammunition.

On 15 May a troop of C Squadron arrested a civilian cycling towards them. Careful interrogation ascertained that he was in fact a Gestapo officer and an SS Lt-Col. Then the squadron discovered a small enemy ammunition dump and destroyed 12 tons of ammunition. The regimental war diaries proudly recorded for 15 May that: 'today was the first occasion on which the Regimental flag was flown in Germany since the day the Regiment was engaged in the occupation of the Rhineland after the Great War.' Much of the rest of May was spent on patrol work, ensuring that German military personnel did not leave the Tonning Peninsula. On 24 May the 8th Hussars established a control post at Norderstapel to assist in the marshalling, disarming and transit of POWs. The following day, Willy's squadron dealt with some 6,000 new German POWs.

By 1 June 1945, C Squadron had moved to Vaale where they were engaged in training and painting their tanks ahead of various victory parades. The first anniversary of D-Day, 6 June 1945, was marked as a holiday with recreational activities for the men, including a regimental dance. On 14 June the regiment received some important news:

> We learned that we were on orders to move shortly to Berlin to carry out escort and guard duties for a month. Of course we knew it had been flattened by Allied bombing. Before we left for Berlin, our leisure activities consisted of a swimming gala in the SS barracks at Gluckstadt. The thought of going to the German capital was exciting for us. I had never been to Berlin before. We couldn't go to Berlin under the Nazis because we had no money then to travel from Bonn.

Tension and excitement mounted when on 1 July, after nearly six weeks in one location, Willy's squadron was at forty-eight hours notice to move to Berlin. An advance party left for Brunswick, and from there moved on Berlin. The following day the 8th Hussars prepared to move in two batches and arrangements made for tanks to be loaded onto transporters. In the early hours of 4 July C Squadron, under the command of Major H.H. Firth, whose tank Willy was driving, loaded their vehicles onto transporters of the Royal Army Service Corps. By 8 a.m. they were on the move to Brunswick and rested overnight at Kirchwege near Uelzen. The rest of the regiment prepared to move the next day. By nightfall the following day, they arrived north of Brunswick with Willy's squadron resting overnight at Rötgesbüttel. Written in the entry of official war diaries is the following comment:

> reports received that Berlin was heavily damaged by bombs and Russian attacks making much of it uninhabitable. The tanks were to be unloaded from transporters and continue the rest of the route on their tracks.

On 7 July the regiment approached Berlin. The long line of tanks and military vehicles moved along the autobahn joining Brunswick with Berlin. At the outskirts of the city, the regiment was met by a military police escort. It was Willy's tank that headed the whole cavalcade. He had the honour of not only driving Major Firth, second-in-command of the squadron, but also of leading the whole regiment into Berlin. Little could he ever have imagined that he would be entering the city in such victorious circumstances.

When we entered Berlin, the devastation around us was so tremendous, almost unimaginable. Everything in front of us was almost destroyed. I noticed that everywhere in the streets, the Germans were looking for people, trying to rebuild their houses, carrying bricks, etc. One could really see how utterly devastated Berlin was. As I drove my tank down those streets, seeing the total destruction before my eyes, it gave me the greatest pleasure to see the city in ruins. This is something which they deserved. After all, they were the aggressors that had perpetrated the most horrendous crimes, as we now know from the full extent of the Holocaust. The worst part about going back to Germany at that time, in both Hamburg and Berlin, was when I spoke to the local people; they were moaning about their own suffering from the bombing. I could not be sympathetic. I always told them, 'You brought this upon yourselves. You were quick in 1933 to become members of the Nazi party and say *Heil Hitler.* You got what you deserved.' Of course they didn't like what I said, but I always made it quite clear to them. But, that did not mean that I would exact revenge on them for my own suffering.

As we entered the city of Berlin, we encountered problems because the Russians made things difficult for us. We had to have the correct papers, etc. and that threatened to hold us up whilst everything was checked. But soon we were on our way into the city. We were escorted to our new billets at the stadium that had been built to house the Olympic Games in Berlin in 1936. Every effort was made to make it habitable.

The Olympischer Platz area leading up to the stadium became a giant 'car park' for the tanks. The official war diaries noted: 'the tanks were an impressive sight when they had formed up bodily upon it [the stadium].' The main difficulty for the men stationed in the stadium was the lack of sufficient fresh water. For drinking and cooking the regiment was entirely dependent on water carts. The city's own water supply had become mixed with the sewage system. Remnants of war was all around, including an unexploded bomb which C Squadron found lodged in the roof of the officers' mess, and gelignite and other explosives in other parts of the barracks. All were dealt with by the Royal Engineers. During his time in Berlin, Willy saw a fair bit of the city:

> The city was a pile of rubble in many parts, a shell of its former glory. Passing the Tiergarten, the city's zoo, the smell was unbearable from the dead animals. The Germans were in a terrible position. They had no cigarettes or coffee, and very little food. In Berlin, they used to follow us when we were smoking a cigarette because they used to pick up the stubs which we threw to the ground. I was much too naive to get involved in the black market there. It was in a special area and I used to go there to watch them. It was possible to sell your cigarettes or rations for a terrible amount of money. The Germans would do anything at that time for cigarettes and coffee. But I never really got myself involved because I couldn't afford to do that. In spite of the utter devastation around us, we managed to have a wonderful time in Berlin. The city was divided into four zones: British, American, French and Russian. We were not allowed to enter the other three zones without special permission.

Spare time was spent around the Kurfürstendamm, one of the most famous parts of Berlin, equivalent to London's Bond Street. Part of the S-Bahn (underground) was still running which enabled Willy and his mates to get to the centre easily. At the end of the Kurfürstendamm was the Gedenk Kirche, the church damaged by Allied bombing which was never rebuilt after the war. It is still standing today, just as it looked when Willy was there in 1945. On one particular day, Willy and his comrades took a trip to the bombed ruins of the bunker where Hitler had committed suicide on 30 April. Willy made a definite decision to see the bunker:

> This was important for me. I had lived for six years under the Nazi regime and experienced brutality at their hands in Dachau. The very thought of Hitler instilled fear into every Jew in Germany at that time. Now, as I stood amongst the ruins of his bunker, the reality dawned on me. Hitler was dead and I had survived. For me it had an extra emotional dimension which did not affect my comrades in the same way.

The result of Hitler's Final Solution to the 'Jewish question' was never far from Willy's mind and experience. In Berlin's former Jewish hospital on Oranienburger Strasse, concentration camp survivors were being brought in daily. It had become a collecting centre where relatives could look for people they thought might have survived any of the concentration camps. Willy visited almost every day:

> I knew that concentration camp survivors were being sent first to the centre at the former Jewish hospital. The plight of these Jews lay heavy on my heart at the time. I visited the place nearly every day, looking out for people I might recognise. I spoke to a lot of them. They were surprised to see me in British army uniform speaking perfect German. I found them in an absolutely terrible condition: very thin, haggard, malnourished and pale, and with deep psychological scars. I was shocked sometimes by just how ill they were. I desperately hoped that I might find my family amongst them but unfortunately no one could tell me anything about them. Then I realised that only ex-Berliners were being sent to the centre. Sooner or later I would have to take a trip to Bonn, but I would have to wait until I was stationed a few weeks later in Lingen.

On 9 July the men prepared for the forthcoming parades. Lorries of each squadron toured what remained of the city and that same day the regimental football team played against a team from 3 Royal Horse Artillery and beat them 4–3. At 6.30 a.m. the following day, the tanks left the tank park and moved down to the Brandenburg Gate. Willy recalls:

> These tank movements were exciting. We formed up four abreast and drove along the road past an improvised saluting base. We had to practise the spacing of tanks. If one moves too fast at the front, larger gaps soon appear between the rows of tanks, and the neat, precise military formation is lost.

The war diaries noted that a distance of 15 yards between rows was apt to increase too much so it was decided to form up at 10 yards between each row of tanks. Another ceremonial practice took place the following day, ahead of the proper ceremony due on 12 July. In the early afternoon of

12 July, the tanks left the tank park and drove to the Brandenburg Gate, taking up their pre-arranged positions. A guard of honour lined the route near the saluting base, consisting of the 8th Hussars, the King's Company 1st battalion, the Grenadier Guards and the 11th Hussars. None other than Commander-in-Chief Field Marshal Sir Bernard Montgomery was presenting a decoration to Russian commanders, Marshals Zhukov and Rokossovsky. Lieutenant Gould and Colonel Hayward were awarded the Military Cross and Military Medal respectively. The war diaries record that: 'The weather was brilliant and a very impressive ceremony took place.'

That evening, the regiment received a message of thanks from Montgomery, who 'wished to express his very great appreciation of the way that all ranks had carried out their duties on the afternoon's parade.' Another parade took place on 13 July down the Charlottenburger Chaussee. From 15 July, all preparations focused on the big victory parade which had been set for Saturday 21 July. Willy comments that 'our tanks had to be in order for that parade. Everything had to be cleaned and our uniforms perfect. It was at this point that we all received our campaign medals.'

The men were woken at 4.30 a.m. on the day of the victory parade. It was to be a long day. After first parade and breakfast, the commanding officer inspected the regiment. At 7.25 a.m. the tanks moved out of the tank park and towards their allocated area in the Charlottenburger Chaussee. They were then formed up quite quickly and the men issued with cups of tea from the cooks' lorries. The grand victory parade began at ten o'clock with an impressive nineteen-gun salute by 3 Royal Horse Artillery. Then Prime Minister Winston Churchill's escort drove in eight half-tracks down the road to inspect the troops on parade. The first consisted of Winston Churchill, Field Marshal Sir Alan Brooke, Field Marshal Sir Bernard Montgomery and Major General L. Lyne. In the second half-track were Admiral of the Fleet Sir Andrew Cunningham, Marshal of the RAF Sir Charles Portal, General of the Army G.C. Marshall, Fleet Admiral E.J. King, General of the Army H.H. Arnold and Field Marshal Sir Harold Alexander. In the third half-track were Field Marshal Sir Henry Maitland Wilson, General Sir Hastings Ismay, The Rt. Hon. Anthony Eden, the Rt. Hon. Clement Attlee, Air Chief Marshal Sir W. Sholto Douglas and Admiral Sir Harold Burrough. The remaining half-tracks carried high-ranking Allied officers and members of government. The whole inspection took forty minutes. At 10.50 a.m. the parade was formed up ready for the march-past which was led by the Royal Navy, HMS *Pembroke*, RN Gunnery School Chatham. The order of march was then:

Headquarters 131 Infantry Brigade
3rd Regiment Royal Horse Artillery
5th Regiment Royal Horse Artillery
8th King's Royal Irish Hussars
11th Hussars
344 Independent SL Battery, Royal Artillery
Royal Engineers, 7th Armoured Division
1st Battalion Grenadier Guards
1/5 Battalion The Queens Royal Regiment
Royal Northumberland Fusiliers
2nd Battalion The Devonshire Regiment
Royal Army Medical Corps & Royal Army Service Corps
Canadian Berlin Battalion

The army troops were followed by the Royal Air Force, and by various military bands who provided the music. Most poignantly, considering all that he had been through and that he was still a German national, Willy took part in the victory parade. He proudly drove his tank crew past Winston Churchill and the Allied leaders for the victory salute.

It was fantastic. We all lined up at the parade ground, and from there it was possible to see all the leaders. There was Winston Churchill standing on a platform. We drove our tanks passed him and other Allied leaders. It remains one of the proudest moments of my life.

After the parade, Prime Minister Winston Churchill opened a NAAFI Club in Berlin, which was named the Winston Club. He ordered that 23 July should be observed as a holiday in gratitude 'to mark the smartness of the Division on the Victory Parade'.

On 1 August the regiment was still in Berlin. That afternoon, a regimental swimming gala and other sports were held in the Olympic Stadium. The war diaries note that C Squadron won. In the coming days, in between training, courses and sport activities, the squadrons were called upon to provide night security guard at the house of the GOC (general officer commanding) at Gatow. The guard consisted of one NCO and six men of other rank. The regiment was also asked to guard an alcohol store in a bombed-out building in the city. They had to contend with the Russians who occasionally tried to offer bribes to obtain bottles of spirits.

On 4 August group photographs were taken of each squadron in front of the Olympic Stadium. During the afternoon the regiment played football against a team from Berlin area HQ and won 10–0. On 13 August Willy moved with his squadron to Itzehoe where tanks were being officially handed over. It was here two days later that news reached them of the unconditional surrender of Japan. The war in the Far East was over.

> We now had high hopes that every aspect of the Second World War was over. It was a time of celebration.

A week later, having dealt with the tanks, C Squadron returned to Berlin. The rest of the month was spent in interior economy and athletics. At the end of August the regiment began its move out of Berlin. Most were sent to Mol in Belgium, approximately 451 miles from Berlin, to begin the conversion to Comet tanks. Willy was posted to Lingen near Munster in Westphalia to begin the training of new tank drivers. For a period of 4–5 weeks, Willy became acting sergeant major while his sergeant major was on a course. It meant a great deal to him:

> It was a wonderful achievement for me. I could tell everybody what to do and when it was time to go on duty, but I never abused my position or overstepped the mark. After all, I always remembered where I came from.

> In Lingen I was in charge of transport. It was also my job to train new recruits to become tank drivers and that included marching and saluting.

I enjoyed it because it brought back so many memories of my own train-ing in Farnborough. It was there then that I was promoted to rank of sergeant. It made a lot of difference because I received more pay, the food was better in the sergeants' mess, and I had my own billets. Every month as a sergeant I was issued with a bottle of whisky or gin. Being a NCO was very important and the comradeship between the sergeants was wonder-ful. As such, I was one of the few Jewish sergeants in the 8th Hussars.

While in Lingen, members of the regiment were given the opportunity to go to a holiday resort on the Friesian Island of Nordeney, off the north coast of Germany, where the best hotels had been requisitioned for the British army. Willy was asked to take twenty of his troopers to Nordeney for a long weekend. It had been a very popular resort for Jews from the Rhineland before the Nazis came to power. Willy's father visited the island on many occasions, but as Willy recalls:

Once the Nazis came to power, they made a lot of propaganda about Nordeney and sent out postcards which read *Nordeney Juden frei* [Nordeney – free of Jews]. It therefore gave me great pleasure that the British had taken over the island at the end of the war and I, as a Jew, was able to have a holiday there. It was no longer *Juden frei*.

On 6 September 1945, exactly a year since the liberation of Ghent, Willy returned briefly to the town to take part in a victory parade. He was accompanied by twenty troopers. It was another historic commemora-tion for Willy, who comments, 'We were looked after very well by the Belgian people and treated with huge respect for our part in the liberation of Ghent the previous year.' He received a certificate dated 6 September 1945 from the town council which reads:

The Town Council and the citizens of Ghent express their real venera-tion and gratitude to the gallant officers and men of the 7th Armoured Division who, on 6th September 1944, delivered our City from the bold and odious German enemy. Glorify the heroic war-acts of the 7th Armoured Division on the African and European continents. Bow deeply for the sacrifices brought by the 7th Armoured Division for the liberty of our City and our Country. Salute in the 7th Armoured Division the spirit of freedom and opposition against all kind of tyranny of the English people, who alone resisted in 1940, the strongest enemy and so made possible the final victory. Long Live the 7th Armoured Division!

After the parade in Ghent, Willy returned to Lingen to continue his transport duties for the regiment, where he remained until his demobilisation the following year. What had not been resolved was the fate of Willy's parents, brother and extended family. From Lingen, he was given a week's compassionate leave by his commanding officer to return to Bonn to look for his parents. He had no idea what had happened to them, although the fate of six million of Europe's Jews in the death camps was now becoming known.

Since Willy was in charge of squadron transport, he was able to take a jeep and drive the 200 miles from Lingen to Bonn. He returned to a city which once had a Jewish community of nearly 1,000 people. Between 1933 and 1939 around 600 had managed to flee Germany and settle in England, Palestine or America, but the remaining 470 perished in the Holocaust. Only eight Jewish citizens of Bonn returned from the concentration camps. Willy now feared the worst for his own family. He comments:

> When I first entered Bonn, it was a strange feeling, but a very emotional one. I had said goodbye to my family from Bonn station back in April 1939. I had not returned since. Walking down the all-too familiar streets brought back floods of childhood memories, both good and bad.

Willy arrived in Bonn late in the evening and made his way straight to the Office of Statistics where all inhabitants were listed:

> The place was closed of course because it was late, but I noticed a night bell for the caretaker. The night man eventually answered. He too was very surprised to see a British sergeant standing in front of him, with revolver, and speaking perfect, fluent German. He told me that nothing could be

done and to return in the morning. I was having none of it. I realised that now I was the master and could command attention. I ordered him to fetch the man in charge immediately. Like a good German, he obeyed. He went off on his bicycle and eventually returned with the man in charge. I was very polite and demanded to see the list of all Jewish persons who had returned to Bonn from concentration camps. They opened the office for me and showed me the lists. Unfortunately, at this early point at the end of the war, only three women and a man were listed as returning from various camps. The man listed was none other than my cousin Rudi Moses! I was surprised and delighted. I noticed that he had been incarcerated in Buchenwald concentration camp but was now in a local hospital. The three women survivors listed happened to be known to me. I hurried back to my billets, determined to visit them the next day.

The following morning, I first visited my cousin in hospital. We were so excited to see each other. I had found one of my relatives. But he couldn't tell me anything of my mother, father, brother and rest of the family. He later emigrated [sic] to America. Then I went to call on the three ladies. When I rang the doorbell, all three came to the door at once. They were shocked and surprised. They almost screamed in delight: 'Willy, *bist du gross geworden!*' [My, Willy, how you have grown!]. They had all been in Theresienstadt. All they could tell me was that the Jewish people of Bonn who were still in Germany in the 1940s were rounded up, taken to a nearby monastery and kept there together for some time. That included my father, my mother, my brother, my uncle and aunt. And that was the last they saw of them.

Willy spent seven days wandering around Bonn, desperately trying to find out something about his family. He visited all the places he and his extended family had ever lived: the Lenné Strasse, Rosen Strasse, Dorotheen Strasse and Reuter Strasse. He saw the bombed-out shell of his father's former shop. At all these places Germans were occupying the houses, but none had ever heard of Willy's family. It was a grim time.

I could find out nothing. Place after place yielded no information. In the Reuter Strasse where my aunt and uncle had lived, only British troops were stationed. At this time, British troops were occupying Bonn. It had been captured by the Americans, but by the time I got there it was in British hands. During these difficult seven days I stayed with other British soldiers in the Reuter Strasse. Ironically I was billeted in a building exactly opposite where my grandmother, aunt and uncle had lived. I went up to the first floor of their old apartment, now occupied by British troops. Of course, nothing was left. All their belongings had long gone. But there was a balcony at the back of the place. I looked out and there on the right-hand side of the balcony was the mangle still standing there. It had been there since I was a young boy. Seeing that one item then brought back all my childhood memories. I also went to a tobacconist shop where I used to buy cigars for my father during the Nazi period and I was so surprised that the woman at the counter recognised me, even in my British army uniform. She said, 'You're the son of Arthur Hirschfeld. I remember you.'

Whilst I was in Bonn at this time I met a gentleman from Belgium who was in charge of the British Control Commission in Germany. He introduced me to a few political members of the German party SPD [Social Democrats]. They asked me to come back to Germany after my demob to join them in politics. I went to one of their meetings but ultimately I had no desire to settle in Germany again. I left Bonn at the end of seven days and returned to my unit with no knowledge of my family or their whereabouts. It was a worrying time.

In April 1946, back in England, Willy's sister received a letter from a stranger with a snippet of news about the family. The letter, originally written in German, is still in Thea's possession. It is dated 15 April 1946 and was from Adele Mange, a survivor of Theresienstadt. Translated from German, the letter reads:

Dear Thea, Your dear relatives, who are here with me at the camp, gave me this letter, so that I can perhaps add something which might interest you. Your dear parents and [brother] Manfred were originally with us in Bonn at Kloster Endenich (originally a convent, then used as a holding centre). From there, we were taken on 24 December 1941 to an old fort in

Koeln-Muengersdorf, where eight of us shared one room. Your parents and Manfred and we [mother and four children] were in a room, which is better described as a cowshed or stable. However, we did the best we could and over Christmas we made a home out of the cowshed. Manfred and we three sisters worked hard together. At any rate, at the time, everyone had a bed and a chair to sit on. Your dear father, who became ill from the outset, was unable to leave his bed and so after a few weeks he was sent to the Jewish asylum in [Koeln-]Ehrenfeld and unfortunately, or perhaps by the grace of God, he died there in March. On 20 July 1942, your mother, Manfred and my dear mother with three of my sisters were then transported eastwards from Cologne, presumably to Minsk, although we were never sure of exactly where the transports were sent.

Where did they all go and what happened to them? Have you or your brother managed to find anything? If so, please do let me know everything. I come from Alfter near Bonn, which you surely must know as you originally come from Bonn. I was taken to Theresienstadt with my dear husband and after 32 months there, we were fortunate enough to have been rescued and escaped to Switzerland, like your dear relatives. If there is anything else you want to know, please do not hesitate to contact me. Best wishes Adele Mange.

It is deeply sad and tragic that Adele Mange did not know of the ultimate fate of the Hirschfelds and may even have hoped that they were still alive. It turns out that around 470 of Bonn's Jews, 35 of them children, were rounded up in 1941 and sent to a Roman Catholic convent. All the nuns had been sent away by the Nazis. On Christmas Eve 1941 they were transferred to an old fort in Koeln-Muengersdorf. There they lived in terrible conditions. The women had to carry out kitchen duties, the men sent out on hard labour. Then in 1942 the Jews of Bonn living in insufferable conditions in the convent were deported to various concentration camps, a number of them to Theresienstadt. In July 1945 only eight Jews of Bonn returned from concentration camps. All the others perished in the Holocaust.

It was only much later that Willy and Thea finally discovered exactly what had happened to their family. Through the Red Cross they learned that their father had died in Cologne awaiting transportation to a concentration camp. Their mother Regina had survived the first camp in Cologne, working as a cleaner for the inmates and earning a little money. She was still able to bury her husband, Willy's father, in May 1942 in the Jewish cemetery in Cologne and provide a headstone on his grave. On 10 July 1942 Regina, along with their brother Manfred, aunt Henriette Moses and uncle Markus Moses, were all taken to Minsk where they were murdered in a concentration camp. Willy and Thea have since conducted searches and received confirmation from records that indeed their family had all perished in a concentration camp near Minsk.

There were thousands of German-speaking refugees in the British forces, like Willy, searching for survivors at the end of the war. Many clung to the last hope that their families would have somehow survived the concentration camps. For many, the news was grim. Most, now as British soldiers, had been into the newly liberated Belsen concentration camp and witnessed firsthand the sheer horror of the camp which haunted them for decades. But there was some good news for Willy's army mate and closest friend Gerry Moore. At the end of the war he was stationed in the Netherlands and received a letter from his father's friend in London that his parents had managed to escape Nazi Germany and had fled to France. They had spent the war in hiding thanks to a Catholic priest in Lyon. Gerry was given compassionate leave by his commanding officer to travel to France to find his parents. He had their last known address and wrote of his coming. He took a train to Lyon to meet his father at the station. Unfortunately, there were three railway stations in Lyon and he arrived at the wrong one. He took a horse and cart and made off for his parents' last address. On the way he saw a gentleman on a bicycle and that was his father. Theirs was an extraordinary reunion, and it was this kind of wartime memory which over the years Willy and Gerry have been able to share with each other.

In December 1946 Willy was demobilised from the army. He was given the opportunity to sign up for another two years and receive promotion but he decided against it. He had had enough and wanted to settle into civilian life. He was now twenty-six. So much had happened to him – almost a lifetime's experience contracted into the seven years since he had left Bonn:

> I would have quite enjoyed being a Sergeant Major, but somehow I felt being interned for a year in Australia followed by five years in the army, it was time to settle down and get on with my life. When I said goodbye to my friends in Lingen, they told me I would be back again in four weeks and that I wouldn't like civvy street, but they were wrong. When I left, I was in charge of ten to fifteen other men who were being demobbed at the same time. I had to take them to Ostend in Belgium where we boarded a boat back to England. I was on leave for the next four to six weeks because of my overseas service. I was still entitled to wear my army uniform during that period. Then the day came for me to report to Olympia in London where I was fitted out with a new suit, shirt, hat and pair of shoes. I was ready for civilian life. I kept just my army jacket and have since donated it to the Jewish Military Museum in Hendon, North-West London where it is on display.

In the first edition of the journal of the 8th King's Royal Irish Hussars to be published after the war, the commanding officer paid tribute to the German-speaking refugees who had served with the regiment. He wrote: 'We were lucky to have in our Squadron a number of German-speaking other ranks, many of whom had had first-hand experience of Nazi brutality.' Willy had served with a number of them. These included Edgar Bender and Dennis Goodman (Hermann Gutmann, born in Frankfurt) who landed with A Squadron of the 8th Hussars on D-Day+3. Dennis served with the regiment in the same front-line battles and campaigns as Willy's squadron, through France, Belgium and Holland, and finally in the invasion of Germany. At the end of the war Dennis was assigned to the Intelligence Corps and the investigation of war crimes at the Neuengamme concentration camp. Dennis and Willy continued to be good friends until Dennis's death in 2007.

Willy also recalls serving in the Royal Armoured Corps with Frank Marshall (Gerhard Silberstein) and H. Barnett, both of whom were captured in action and taken as POWs. They spent time in POW camp

Stalag IVD in Germany. It is believed that they survived because they had anglicised their names and their original German identity was never discovered by the Nazis.

Over sixty years later, the memories of those unprecedented years continue to have an impact on Willy. There is not a day which passes when he does not think about some aspect of those days – of life under Nazism, haunted memories of Dachau, or his time in Australia or serving in the British army, but for all that he has gone through, he can still say this:

I am no hero. Circumstances dictated my life. That was certainly true of Dachau and Australia. I had no choice. After Australia, I did have a choice and I decided to join the Pioneer Corps and then the 8th King's Royal Irish Hussars. For all the suffering and hardship, I couldn't exact revenge on the Germans I met at the end of the war. It was my aim to finish the war and have peace.

CHAPTER 10

CIVILIAN LIFE AND FOR THE LOVE OF ARSENAL

Having been demobbed and returned to England, Willy was under no illusion about the difficulties of adjusting to civilian life after the war. He had little formal training, having had his education disrupted by the Nazi regime in Germany. The first priority was to find somewhere to live, which he did, taking a furnished room in Swiss Cottage, North-West London. It was initially a very lonely time because all his friends who had been with him in Australia were still in the army. They had not yet been demobbed. The Swiss Cottage area of North-West London became an important focus for the lonely twenty-six-year-old Willy. The area became a hub of Continental life, a microcosm of German and Austrian society, where English could be heard with a heavy German or Viennese accent. It was here that he could find his feet and begin to establish a normal life:

When I first came out of the army, I was very lonely for the first three to four weeks. The Finchley Road in Swiss Cottage was a place I could wander around and meet people I knew from army days or other refugees. The Finchley Road was often colloquially called Finchley Strasse! Some of the bus conductors would call out 'Swiss Cottage austeigen!' at the station. Around the corner was the famous Continental restaurant the

Cosmo owned by ex-Austrian refugees, which was the main meeting place along with the Lyons tea house for the refugees. The Cosmo was where I met a lot of my old friends again. The food was really excellent – good German and Austrian cuisine.

The other important place for Willy at this time was the ex-servicemen's club in Circus Road, St John's Wood. He spent his leisure time and some evenings there, again mixing with ex-refugees, all of them having served in the British forces. Gradually most of his friends had been demobbed from the army and were trying to adapt to civilian life. They also found it difficult. A Jewish football club, Bar Kochba, was in existence at this time in North-West London. Eventually Willy and his friends (Gerry and Joe) joined the club and during the football season they played against other teams, especially in the Kilburn league. Most Sunday mornings they played in either Hackney Marshes, Lyttleton Road or Vale Farm in Wembley. Willy comments:

> Our girlfriends and wives attended matches to cheer us on and we became quite a group, also meeting regularly at each others' houses. It was quite a social network. Tennis was another game I enjoyed playing to keep fit.

The sport gave a light relief during the years immediately after the war when the challenges of civilian life proved difficult. Willy's friend Joe Milton went into the jewellery trade; Herbert Bright emigrated to America; Franzl Bartes emigrated to Canada, and Kurt Morgenroth became Willy's business partner. Willy's closest friend Gerry Moore worked initially in London in the export trade, eventually turning his hand to the metal trade.

Having sorted out his accommodation, Willy himself turned to finding a job. It was not going to be easy to get established in any trade. He contacted a sergeant who had been in the Royal Electrical and Mechanical Engineers, who had been demobbed at the same time. Together they set up a car repair business in Enfield, but it was a rough time:

> We had difficulties from the beginning. We couldn't get spare parts for the cars and we didn't get customers either so we had to give up.

Then I started with someone else as a travelling salesman, selling anything we could – from teddy bears to corkscrews. That didn't work either. I spent more time in the Lyons tea houses than selling goods. Then I had a chance to start with my former boss from Germany Mr Hearst [originally Mr Herz]. He had a chemical factory in Wales but I didn't want to go to Wales; I wanted to stay in London. So I didn't do that either.

Personal contacts were vital at this time. Willy then eventually came across an older friend, Kurt Morgenroth, who had been with him in internment in Australia and then the Pioneer Corps, but had been invalided out of the Pioneer Corps after four weeks when a concrete mixer fell on his leg. Kurt had returned to London and learnt the trade of watchmaker. When the war was over, he started importing watches from Switzerland and began a mail-order business. He met Willy one day and asked him to join him at his premises in Gray's Inn Road. Willy took up work for him on an initial wage of £10 a week. The business became successful and expanded until it had several jewellery shops. Willy was eventually made a partner and worked in the trade for twenty-two years:

> In 1969 the business was taken over by a public company. This changed everything. I didn't like it at all once it had become a public company. I left and started up on my own … Eventually I became the sole UK agent for a company called Gundlach, which traded in diaries and advertising gifts. I finally retired from there at the age of eighty in 2000.

Life was not all work in those days. By chance in 1946, Willy met the woman who would become his wife. At the time he was lodging in Buckland Crescent, Swiss Cottage, when again he met another friend whom he had been with in Australia, who had also been in the British army. He asked Willy where he lived and was surprised to discover that they lived opposite each other. Willy recalls:

> He told me that he lived with a lady friend on the first floor of the place opposite me and it would be great to come and meet her and have

a coffee. That lady turned out to be my future mother-in-law. I accepted the invitation to coffee and it was then that I met her daughter Judy. They were also originally refugees, and that afternoon I was told their whole remarkable, but sad story. We became very close, Judy and I. She was just fifteen at the time.

Judy was born Jutta Fabian in Berlin in March 1932 to Else and Herbert Fabian. Her father never got out of Nazi Germany and eventually perished in Auschwitz. Judy left Berlin in July 1939 with her mother and brother Manfred (Peter) and came to England on a domestic visa. Her mother had originally had some difficulty getting papers that would include her children. It took approximately six months to secure a permit for them and, little did they realise then, but it was a 'false' visa. They had come under the protection of Frank Foley, head of MI6 in Berlin operating out of the British Passport Control Office there. Between 1932 and 1939 he faked documentation which enabled at least 10,000 Jews to get out of Germany. His efforts have now been recognised with the erection of two monuments to his memory and granted status as 'A Righteous Gentile' at Yad Vashem, Israel's Holocaust Museum. It is now known that Judy, her mother and brother were among the Jews that Frank Foley saved. Judy still has her original German passport which has been stamped by Frank Foley's office, dated 22 June 1939. She and her brother came out on a domestic permit as a married couple, even though they were only aged seven and ten at the time. Judy explains:

We always suspected that Frank Foley had something to do with it. We sailed for England on an American ship. We never knew who paid for us. We needed a guarantor, money even for a domestic permit. The benefactor was never revealed. We now know that it is possible that Frank Foley forged figures on our original application forms to say that money had been deposited on our behalf into a bank. When we arrived in England we went straight to the family where we were listed on our visas to go as a domestic. This was somewhere in Essex. When we arrived at the house, there was already a refugee family living there with exactly the same names and details as us. There was a mother, daughter and brother who had come out as a married couple. We had both been issued with identical 'false' papers by Frank Foley.

When war broke out, Judy was separated from her mother and taken into a foster family. It was the beginning of several years of insecurity and uncertainty for the young Judy as she was sent from foster home to foster home. First she was in Torquay, South Devon for a few weeks, then Coventry, Wakefield and finally Abbots Langley in Hertfordshire where she attended the local school.

After the war, at the age of thirteen, Judy returned to live with her mother. Having met Willy at the age of fifteen, they struck up a close friendship and fell in love. In 1947 Willy became a British citizen. It was what he had always hoped for since first arriving in England nine years earlier. The first thing he was determined to do was apply for a British passport. This was terribly important to him.

> When I applied to become a British citizen, I had to appear before a Tribunal. There was no difficulty with that. It all went very smoothly, but I was surprised to learn that the panel knew all about me, including my army career. I was granted British citizenship. I had a tremendous respect for the country which had saved my life, and to be a citizen of that country was the greatest honour. Having a British passport crowned it all.

Even though Willy was now a British citizen, Judy's mother would not permit him to marry Judy until he had somewhere suitable for them to settle down. He spent the next couple of years getting his life together and establishing himself in steady employment. On 29 March 1949, at the age of twenty-eight, Willy married his seventeen-year-old bride at Hampstead Registry Office, North London. A local rabbi, who was also a friend, performed a religious ceremony under a *chuppah* (canopy) that same afternoon in Judy's mother's flat. They were surrounded by their friends:

> It was a wonderful occasion. We were, and still are, very happy together. Although it was nearly two years after the war, rationing was still in force. We did the best we could for the food afterwards. With the help of friends

who shared their rations with us, we managed to provide enough food for everyone the whole day. We spent our honeymoon for two nights in the Cumberland Hotel, Marble Arch at 21s. a night. We returned to live in a bed-sit room in Merton Rise, Swiss Cottage area of North-West London.

That same year, just after they were married, Willy and Judy travelled to Bonn together. They visited the grave of Arthur Hirschfeld who had died in Cologne in May 1942 awaiting transportation to a concentration camp. 'I was so surprised,' says Willy, 'that my mother had been determined enough to put a headstone on my father's grave. After all, it was not that easy under the Nazis.' The headstone reads:

> Here lies my beloved husband,
> our good father,
> Arthur Hirschfeld
> Born 16 April 1879
> Died 15 May 1942

In April 1954 Willy was officially told by letter, from the Jewish congregation of Cologne, about the fate of his mother, brother, aunt and uncle. He was able to put a plaque on his father's grave in memory of those who had perished in Minsk because they have no known grave.

Willy and Judy soon settled into married life. In those early days they, like many Continentals, frequented the shops and coffee houses of Swiss Cottage. Just before Christmas 1949, they were able to move to a small garden flat off Finchley Road in Greencroft Gardens. In 1951 their first son David was born, followed by Anthony in 1954. That same year Willy and his family moved to a large house, also in North-West London.

Apart from his wife and family, Willy has another lifelong love which goes way back to his childhood – football. It was the most important sport during the Hitler years because he could only play in a Jewish team before that too was outlawed by the regime. He comments:

Already, during the Hitler years, I had heard about the famous Arsenal football team. We didn't have a television back in 1935/6, but that year I remember reading a lot about Arsenal in the Nazi newspapers. I formed a high opinion of the team, little knowing then that events would unfold that would lead to my emigration to England and becoming one of the team's longest-running supporters.

When Willy came to England in 1939, he attended his first Arsenal match which was to mark the beginning of his seventy-year love affair with the club. During the year of internment in Australia, football again became an important activity, as it did during his service in the British army. After the war, Willy and his two ex-refugee army friends Joe and Gerry had high aspirations of becoming Arsenal season-ticket holders. They attended as many matches as they could. When it came to applying for a season ticket for 1947/8, they wrote to the secretary of the club explaining that they had just been demobbed, had spent six years in the army and fought on the front line in Europe, and now would love to have an Arsenal season ticket. They were in luck. The reply came back and they received three season tickets. They were allocated seats at the west end Block U, row J, seats 21, 22 and 23 at the old ground at Highbury. Willy recalls:

> The cost of the season ticket then was £7 10s. per season ticket. It enabled us to watch all the first League matches and the reserve matches. It also included extra coupons towards payment for the Cup Finals which were extra, plus a renewal form for the next season. We knew then that we were Arsenal season-ticket holders for as long as we wanted it. I had the same seat until the last game at Highbury against Wigan in 2005/6.

Eventually, Willy's friends Joe and Gerry gave up their seats, which enabled Willy's two sons David and Anthony to take them over. For the last forty years, David and Anthony have attended matches with their father. Willy has attended some of the most exciting matches. He was present at the game in 1948 when Arsenal won the First Division title; also 1950 when they won the FA Cup at Wembley against Liverpool. The latter was a memorable match as Willy recalls: 'I stood with Gerry and Joe behind the goal. We had a great position for the game, but unfortunately

Gerry had broken his leg playing football six weeks earlier and was still in plaster. We had to hold him up for most of the match!' Willy was also at the last domestic match in 1958 against Manchester United, before tragedy struck the team. He remembers:

> It was another tremendously exciting match. We lost 5–4 but the famous Busby Babes were playing for Manchester United. Sadly it was to be their last game on British soil because five days later they were killed in the Munich air crash. Five of the Busby Babes were killed. It was a tragic moment for one of the finest football teams in England.

Willy was to witness some triumphant moments with the Arsenal team. In 1970/1 Bertie Mee became Arsenal's new manager. In the first season with him, the team clinched their first double. They beat their rivals Tottenham 1–0 at White Hart Lane and won the League Title; then they defeated Liverpool 2–1 at Wembley to claim the Cup Final. 'I was lucky,' comments Willy, 'to have been at all these matches.'

In 1997/8 Arsène Wenger became the new Arsenal manager. In his first season at Highbury he took the club to a double victory. Arsenal won the FA Cup and the League. Their third double victory came in 2001/2 when again they claimed the FA Cup and the League. The season 2003/4 was a triumphant one for Arsenal when they won back the title Premiere League Champions in unbeatable fashion, managing to go through the entire season without a single defeat. The season 2005/6 was Arsenal's last at Highbury because they had a new state-of-the-art ground – the Emirates Stadium. With the move from Highbury to the Emirates, Willy, his sons and grandsons are now seated in the Upper Tier, row 7. He reflects:

> I was sorry when we left Highbury because I had become so friendly with the seat-holders all around us. However, Arsenal really needed a high-class stadium with a capacity of 60,000. The new stadium is fantastic. I am still fit enough to walk down the steps at the end of a game. I will carry on going each week to the Emirates Stadium for as long as I can. Now we have five seats and I go with my sons and grandsons.

Willy's long support of Arsenal was officially recognised in 2005 when he received a personal letter from the manager Arsène Wenger. It is dated 28 November 2005:

Dear Willy,

I would like to take this opportunity to thank you for your long and loyal support of Arsenal Football Club which I can assure you has been much appreciated by all players and staff over the years. As you can imagine we have been delighted with the team's recent domestic achievements and are now hoping that season 2005/06, our last at Highbury, will prove to be both successful and enjoyable for everyone concerned. I am enclosing a signed photo, together with our latest squad card and an individual pen picture, and would ask you to accept these items with my compliments. We look forward to your continued interest and support of the Club and I send you my kindest personal regards and all good wishes for the future.

Signed: Arsène Wenger.

Willy's support for Arsenal is impressive. He has been a season-ticket holder of the club since 1947/8 and a supporter for seventy years. He has attended nearly 1,700 matches on home ground and Cup matches, but his interest in football extends beyond Arsenal. He has witnessed firsthand some of the most exciting games in football history, including the World Cup Final at Wembley in 1966 when Germany played England. That year he had a season ticket for all the World Cup matches at Wembley:

It was an exciting game. The most memorable part was when the Russian linesman awarded England the goal when everyone wondered whether or not it was over the line. In the row in front of me were some young German supporters. They cheered when Germany scored the first goal. They thought Germany would win and had got the champagne ready, but England beat Germany 4–2. At the end the German supporters in front of me turned around and shared their champagne with me. I was very happy with the result. I supported England because I am now British after all.

The events which shaped Willy's life as a newly arrived refugee were never far from his mind, even in peacetime. He and Judy are members of the Association of Jewish Refugees (AJR). Judy has been a volunteer for over twenty-five years at Cleve House in West Hampstead, a day centre run by the AJR. In 1980 a *Dunera* Europe Association was founded by former 'Dunera boys', with Dr Fred Parkinson as chairman, Peter Eden as deputy chairman and Rudy Karrell as secretary. The first meeting took place at the Plaza Eden Hotel, Kensington (owned by Peter Eden) with over a hundred *Dunera* boys and their wives attending. Willy became a member and regularly attended meetings; he eventually became part of the committee. Later, the Association met once a year at Garbo's Restaurant with the aim of providing a social gathering of those who had been in internment in Australia. Willy recalls one unique meeting:

> In 1994 we met for a special lunch to celebrate fifty years of the D-Day landings. It gave us so much pride to commemorate this day because most of our *Dunera* boys had served in the British forces during the war. We all wore our campaign medals and celebrated in style at Garbo's Restaurant.

The Association carried on for nearly twenty years until dwindling numbers forced it to dissolve. Only a few *Dunera* boys are left in London. They now belong to The *Dunera* Association, Australia which is still very active and produces a quarterly newsletter.

Willy has made the most of his life. In March 2009 he and Judy celebrated their Diamond wedding anniversary with family and friends. For a couple aware of their German roots but who are, and feel, totally British, it was a proud moment to receive a telegram of congratulations from the Queen on their special day. They were able to look around them with pride that day at the successes of their sons and grandchildren. Their eldest son David is a chartered accountant, and son Anthony is UK sales manager for Gundlach Packaging (Oerlinghausen, Germany), for which Willy once worked. Having lost all his family in the Holocaust, except his twin sister Thea, family life remains terribly important to Willy. The continuity of the family line is something which has been ensured through his sons Anthony and David, seven grandchildren and three great-grandchildren. He says:

I only wish my dear father and mother could know that we are all OK, that her family has survived and continues for the next three generations at least. Knowing that Thea and I were safe in England before she died in the camp, she could assume that the family line would survive through us. And in surviving, we refuse to grant Hitler a posthumous victory.

CHAPTER 11

RETURN TO DACHAU

Over the years, memories of Dachau continued to haunt Willy in quiet moments. In the summer of 1980 Dr Hans Daniels, the Oberbürgermeister (mayor) of Bonn, invited all former Jewish citizens back to the city for a reunion. Willy received a letter, originally in German, in June 1980 from the mayor:

> The town of Bonn has the great pleasure to invite you to visit your home town. We people of Bonn know that it would be very difficult for you to return because of all the dreadful memories but we would like to show our friendship and reconciliation. We would like to reach out to you and hope that you will accept our invitation. Once we know that you are coming, we will inform you of all the details. Goodbye and we hope to see you in Bonn. Yours Dr Hans Daniels.

Willy took the decision to go with his wife Judy, a trip which was fully funded by the city of Bonn. He comments:

> Bonn was still the capital of the Republic of Germany at this time. It was a great honour and I was so pleased that I accepted the invitation because

around 120 people attended the gathering. All were ex-Bonners, some with their wives and husbands who came from all over the world: America, South Africa, Israel, Holland, Britain and France. I was reunited with so many good old friends of mine who I went to school with, including those who I didn't know had survived the Holocaust. It was wonderful to learn that they were still alive. At this reunion, I also met my former teacher from the Jewish school in Bonn, Hans Hammerstein. He had also been on the *Dunera* to Australia but I didn't know it at the time. Once in Australia, I saw him from a distance when the 2,000 internees were split into two groups: he went to Camp 7 and I to Camp 8. We waved at each other and I knew then that he had survived. At the reunion in Bonn in 1980, Hans Hammerstein was reunited with quite a few of his former Jewish pupils, including me. We were able to catch up on the lost years. Photographs subsequently appeared in the local German press. It was also the week of the annual Beethoven festival and we were invited to the famous Beethoven concert hall for the performance of his 9th Symphony. It was a very powerful and moving occasion.

It was such a successful reunion that it became an annual event. The city of Bonn has welcomed its former Jewish residents back for the last thirty years, with Willy and his wife taking the opportunity to fly to Bonn every summer.

In 1981 Willy and other former Jewish Bonners were invited by the German President Karl Carstens and the Chancellor Helmut Schmidt to the Palais Schaumburg in Bonn for a reception. In 1986 the reception took place in the Villa Hammerschmidt at the invitation of the then president Dr Ernst Albrecht. On that occasion Willy gave the vote of thanks on behalf of the former Jewish citizens of Bonn and was photographed with Dr Albrecht and Dr Hans Daniels. In his speech, originally in German, Willy told the gathering:

In the name of all the Jewish visitors I would like to thank you from my heart for your wonderful words and hospitality. As always the Oberbürgermeister Dr Daniels and his staff have excelled themselves in the organisation and programme. My wife and I are here for the seventh time and we feel quite at home. That we come back every year is a testimony to the welcome we have had. I reach my hand out to you this time and on behalf of this group, I thank you very much.

Willy and Judy are still in touch with their former Jewish friends from Bonn. Reflecting after these visits Willy is able to say: 'at least I have the satisfaction of knowing that the Germans today have realised the terrible things committed during the Nazi era and are making gestures of reconciliation for the past. I believe now that the German nation will never again perpetrate such horrendous crimes against Jews and humanity.'

Then in 1997 Willy was invited to visit the children at the Hauptschule St Hedwig, a Roman Catholic school in Bonn. At the time, the schoolchildren were aged ten and eleven. He spoke about his life under the Nazis, time spent in Dachau and in the British army:

They were already very well prepared by their school teacher, so I decided to talk about my life story rather than the Holocaust in general. They were so interested in what I had to say that I was invited again the following year. It became an annual event. Over the years we have developed a very special friendship.

The teacher, Gabriele Wasser, has written about their unique relationship for this book:

I first met Willy in the week of friendship with the former Jewish citizens of Bonn. In the first years, Willy didn't want to go to meet the children in the school as a witness of the Holocaust. It took me a few years to convince him. In 1997 we started a project with ten-year-old pupils in a vocational school in Bonn. As a teacher I'm convinced that learning about the Holocaust has to start very early. After some time, Willy agreed to join me in my school. Before Willy's visit I gave the children a good background understanding about Judaism and the time of the Nazis. Willy and I discussed what he was going to tell them. We started with stories about his childhood. We heard about his love of sport, especially football, about his friends, school life and things in the interest of ten-year-old kids.

Step after step we started to speak also about the excluding of the Jewish people from society. Willy has a wonderful way of reaching the minds of the kids. The first meeting was very emotional. In the time when Willy was not in Germany we had some lessons about Anne Frank and Janusz Korzcak. The pupils wrote letters and postcards to Willy to inform him about their lives. The following year, they became more experienced and older to understand different stories. I gave the historical background of the years 1933–1939. In that time Willy spoke about the restrictions from the Nazis on the Jewish population in Bonn and how he was affected by that. One of Willy's original friends Mrs Gerda Wiener also told the stories from a girl's point of view. In that week the children met also some former Jewish members of Bonn and conducted some interviews. Later they wrote reports about it.

After Willy's visit, the children took some public action against recent displays of Nazism. They didn't allow a famous artist to put a painting of Adolf Hitler next to a painting of Anne Frank and Albert Einstein, near the airport of Cologne. They collected 3,000 signatures from people in the streets of Bonn and wrote a letter to the president of Germany and the mayor of Bonn. They were successful with that. The artist had to take the painting down. The children were very proud of what they did. They did it because Willy had touched their senses. The year after, Willy told the children about Dachau camp and about his life in the war. Like all the years before the children were instructed about the background.

In 2000, after Willy had spoken to the children at the Hauptschule St Hedwig, a lady by the name of Gisela Steinhauer came up to him and asked whether he would be willing to be interviewed on the German radio station WDR5. She had an hourly programme every day called *Tisch Gespräch* (table talk). She was interested in his life story and arranged to visit him in London in February 2000, during which time she interviewed him for over an hour at his home. The programme was broadcast in Germany on 20 April 2000 from 2 p.m. to 3 p.m. and was repeated on the evening of 25 April. During that programme Willy was asked to choose a special piece of music for the air. He chose Al Jolson singing 'April Showers'.

That year was to be special for Willy: on 17 August 2000 he turned eighty years old. The special friendship which he had built up with Gabriele Wasser and the pupils at Hauptschüler St Hedwig was to lead to some extraordinary events at the turn of the millennium. The German schoolchildren decided to surprise him with a visit to London especially for his eightieth birthday. Gabriele Wasser writes:

In August 2000 the pupils planned to do something for Willy's 80th Birthday and we decided to take a coach to visit Willy at his home in London. We planned the visit with Judy and it was a complete surprise for Willy. It was very important for the kids to visit Willy on his birthday. After the long experience from the children with Willy and his life, they wanted to do something unusual for his 80th. We chartered a coach and drove the whole night to London. We walked through the streets of London with our presents, a self composed birthday song and a big banner with 'Happy Birthday Willy'. It was a wonderful surprise for Willy. That day made the relationship between the kids and Willy much stronger. In the years after, Willy spoke with the older children more and more about his loss in the Holocaust and the war. He also spoke about his new beginning in England.

Then in 2001 Gabriele Wasser asked Willy if he would accompany her and the schoolchildren on a trip to Dachau concentration camp. She recalls:

The children had come to see Willy as their own grandfather and they were very shocked about what had happened in the camps. They asked him to join them on a class study trip to Dachau. Willy had his doubts and he told the children that he would give them the answer in a couple of days. At last he agreed. So we planned the tour for the end of 2001.

It was a courageous decision. Physically being back in Dachau on a visit would bring all kinds of painful memories to the fore. At a distance in England he could deal with his experiences, but going back to the actual camp was a different matter. He would be in the place where he had suffered so much in the four long months of his incarceration at the hands of the Nazis. Willy states:

> This was a difficult decision for me because I had not been anywhere near Dachau since my release in 1939. I agreed to go, and in December 2001 my wife Judy and I accompanied them to Dachau concentration camp. I adjusted to the idea of going back there and I didn't worry about it. The camp had most impact on Judy. She didn't like seeing the parade ground where terrible atrocities had taken place.

The archivist at the museum at Dachau found Willy's original papers and entry in the ledger from when he had first arrived there on 15 November 1938. Willy recalls of that momentous visit:

> It was a lousy day when I returned to Dachau. The terrible parade ground was there - bringing back floods of memories of our roll-call and the 2–3 days and nights when we had had to stand in the freezing weather because one person was missing. Now there is a museum on the site of the camp. The lady attending the museum brought out the original ledger which showed the handwritten entry with my name and the date that I was taken into the concentration camp. It was eerie for my wife and me to see that original entry. But somehow it did not affect me that much. What affected me was the way that the huts had been recreated and sanitised. But how else could it be sixty years later?

The visit to Dachau made a lasting impression on the school. Gabriele Wasser recently wrote of it:

> Willy and Judy flew from London to Munich and they joined us for three days. Willy showed the pupils the place where he was in Dachau and told them about the daily life of the prisoners there. The kids became very emotional and they started to realise what had happened in the camps. They understood the great sacrifice that Willy made for them and they understood better what happened to the Jews in the time of the Nazis. When we came to the archive of Dachau, Willy stood suddenly in front of

the name list of Dachau prisoners and he saw his own name and number again. He was stunned and the moments of his imprisonment in Dachau became a reality again. At that moment I was not sure that I did the right thing in bringing him back to this place. After the visit to the archive we made a short ceremony in the synagogue of Dachau, another very emotional moment. All the emotions were too much for all of us, so we drove to the city of Munich and spend some hours on the Christmas Market. After a few hours on the market, Willy told me and the kids that he was glad that he went with us to show us the camp. In the 2002 when the children finished school, they invited Willy and Judy to their party on a boat on the Rhine. In their speech they told Willy and Judy how important his visits in school were and how much they took of them for the rest of their life.

The visit had been of mutual benefit. Its legacy on a new generation lasting, as Gabriele Wasser expresses:

The long relationship that the children had with Willy changed their way of thinking about other people, races and religions and made them more tolerant. In all those years the class members took part of the ceremonies of the '*Kristallnacht*' in Bonn because they thought that we are not allowed to forget the things what happened at that time. After this long personal experience with Willy and Judy I feel myself a part of Willy's family. The project with Willy was for me the most important work that I did with the children in my whole period of service as a teacher.

In 2007 a museum was opened in Bonn which records the history of the Jews in the Rhineland. One of the displays is about Willy's life and that of his family, including photographs and texts about family members who perished in the Holocaust. Willy and Judy are honorary members of the museum.

A lifetime has passed since the days of Hitler and Nazism in Germany. In the interim, Willy has dealt with many painful ghosts from the past, but how does he feel about Germans today?

It can be too easy to harbour resentment, but that is destructive. I am not a vindictive person. I can forgive people but I will never forget what happened. One cannot blame the children or grandchildren of today for what happened under the Nazis. However, I do think about what their parents or their grandparents were doing in the 1930s. How can I not? I will always hate the time from 1933 until 1939. But the world has changed. Germany is not what it was then. It has become a democratic civilised country.

In retirement, Willy continues to lead an active life. Apart from regularly attending Arsenal football matches, he keeps in touch with old army mates. Each month, a group of around a dozen ex-Pioneers meet in a coffee shop in North-West London and reminisce about their wartime service. Amongst them are Harry Rossney, Hans Jackson, Peter Eden, Rudy Karrell, Frank Berg, John Langford, Geoffrey Perry, Bill Howard, Ralph Fraser and Leo Dorffman. Willy is also still in touch with his oldest army friend Gerry Moore who now lives in Paris. They communicate by telephone every week and visit each other once a year. 'After every Arsenal match,' says Willy, 'I have to ring him to give him the result. It's important for us to keep in touch, after all, our friendship goes back to 1940.'

In the summer of 2006 Willy was invited by BBC South-West to go back to Ilfracombe in North Devon where he had trained in the Pioneer Corps in 1941. It was the first time he had been back for sixty-five years. He returned with fellow veterans Geoffrey Perry, Harry Rossney and Fritz Lustig. The purpose was to make a short documentary for BBC South-West's popular *Inside Out* programme produced by Mick Catmull. They were able to walk down memory lane, past all the familiar places which had been part of their life back then: along the promenade where they had carried out daily marching practice; into the Osborne Hotel where they had been billeted; the Alexandra Theatre where they had watched so many shows by other Continentals in the army. Finally they headed for the quaint harbour, where they had once practised defending the town against an invading force. The documentary was screened on 16 October 2006 and again on Armistice Day that year.

In February 2009 Willy was one of the veterans interviewed for a documentary based on the author's book *The King's Most Loyal Enemy Aliens*, filmed by True North Productions for the National Geographic Channel. The documentary was entitled *Churchill's German Army* and was shown worldwide on 26 April 2009. The film crew and production team flew Willy to Eindhoven on 10 February for a two-day schedule of filming. For the first time in over sixty years he was taken back to the place where his tank was knocked out by the railway line between Eindhoven and Nijmegen. He recalls:

It was not easy to find the exact spot after so long. It was September 1944 that I was last in that area, but the railway line was still there, although it was now disused. It did not bother me to be standing there. What affected me more was visiting the grave of one of my comrades afterwards. Having filmed along the railway line and explained what had happened that day, I was driven by the film crew to Meirlo British war cemetery not far away. It is here that my wireless operator John Gardner was buried after he died on the way to the first-aid station. It was he that I had pulled out of the burning tank. I have always treasured the letter which his parents wrote to me after his death and it is something I get out of the drawer and read from time to time. It was always my wish to visit his grave at some point during my lifetime. Now just eighteen months from my nintieth birthday, I was making this special trip. As I walked through the cemetery, memories flooded back. I lost all my crew that day. I approached his grave, deeply moved finally to see his name incised in neat lettering on the headstone with the crest of the 8th Hussars. It was a very emotional moment for me as I bent down and laid flowers at the foot of his grave. It was to be expected that the memories of that dreadful day would vividly surface, but it also gave me great satisfaction that at last I had visited his grave. It shook me because he was just twenty-three years old. I had had the good fortune to survive the war and live a full life with a family. As I left the cemetery, I signed the visitors book – another significant moment for me.

On 4 September 2007 Willy was one of over 250 veterans who gathered at London's Imperial War Museum to celebrate the contribution which the refugees from Nazism made to the British forces in the Second World War. The reunion was organised by Suzanne Bardgett and her team at the Holocaust Exhibition Office of the museum. Veterans came from all over Britain but also America, Austria, Belgium, France and South Africa. In the opening address on that memorable occasion, Field Marshal Lord Bramall paid tribute to the men and women, like Willy Field, who had sacrificed their freedom to liberate Europe from Nazism. He told the gathering:

As I am sure I do not have to tell you, you are a quite remarkable group. Uprooted from your homes in Germany and Austria in the 1930s, you found refuge in this country, and went on to serve Britain and ultimately to bring victory to the Allied cause. Your story is an extraordinary and singular aspect of Allied victory over Nazi Germany ... You were the lucky ones who managed to get temporary visas to get out of Nazi Germany and Austria, your families having been ostracised from professions, schools and even public places by the Nazi anti-Jewish laws. A good many of you came as child refugees, on the kindertransports, leaving your parents behind on what turned out to be the eve of the Second World War. As youngsters, you adopted the English language for everyday use, and fitted into the homes and schools that you found here. Others of you were eighteen or nineteen when you arrived.

Then in 1940 your circumstances changed. Many of you were interned during the Invasion Scare, the wartime government being fearful of Fifth Columnists who might be seeking to betray the country from within. Perverse it may have been to imprison people who had themselves fled Hitler, but it reflected the concerns of the day, and I believe that there was happily a ready understanding of this by the refugees themselves.

Once the authorities had realised that there was a distinction to be made between enemy aliens who were a danger to national security, and those who had actually fled Nazi tyranny, opportunities to serve in the forces opened up, and this is where your contribution to Allied Victory began to take shape ... And with your firsthand knowledge of the Nazi regime, you knew better than we did the deplorable depths to which Hitler and his henchmen could sink. You knew all too well that the new regime signified loss of liberty, overt persecution and worse. And so you were determined to fight that regime with all your might …

I know that you will all have memories of the extraordinary comradeship which develops between soldiers, but that these of course are tinged with great regret at the loss of many promising young lives. And so we remember also today those of your comrades who did not come back: those who fell in battle or who, having been dropped behind enemy lines, were ambushed, captured and killed. The campaign which followed the Normandy Landings saw thousands killed in action, and many who should rightfully be here today lost their lives at that crucial time. And then there were numerous special missions – both secret and dangerous – for which your comrades laid down their lives.

It was a unique gathering that day, and the first time that these veterans had received national recognition for their part in the Second World War. Willy was one of five veterans invited to address the gathering. It was also an opportunity to reflect and remember fellow refugees who had not survived the war but who had lost their lives on the battlefields of Europe.

Given his extraordinary survival against the odds, Willy is in no doubt that serving in the British forces was the right action. He could have spent the duration of the war in the relative safety of England or Australia, but he chose a different path. He expresses the sentiments of so many refugees who joined the forces – this was *his* war:

I knew what it was like to lose one's freedom. It is so easy today to take for granted that we live in a democracy, but back in the Hitler years there was no freedom. The state controlled your lives, there was no freedom of speech, and for me as a Jew that meant virtually becoming invisible, not existing. It became a terrifying regime to live under. You never knew whether you would live or die. Terror and fear were all around you. Knowing this as I did, I saw it as unquestionably my duty to fight in the British forces – to fight for the country that had saved my life. Hitler could not be allowed to win. That would have meant total disaster. I wanted to give something back to the country which had saved my life.

Willy has lived in Britain for over seventy years, a full life and one that is totally loyal to the Crown. He has a deep-rooted pride in being British and that includes having served in the 7th Royal Armoured Division, a regiment with such an honoured reputation. Over those seventy years he has supported his favourite football team – Arsenal. You can't really get more British than that. And in a way, like so many refugees from Nazism who came to this country, he is more British than British. He concludes:

> For all the risks, I never regretted having been part of the biggest invasion force to land in Normandy back in June 1944, but it inevitably brought personal losses. We were young at the time and got on with what we had to do. Hitler had to be defeated – there was no other option in my mind.
>
> I am very proud to have served in the 8th King's Royal Irish Hussars. There was wonderful comradeship which is something I will always remember. As a refugee from Nazi oppression, I am happy that I served England which had, after all, given me my freedom. For this I am very grateful. I feel absolutely British and not at all German, even though I was born and raised in Germany for the first eighteen years of my life. I have no difficulty with going back to Germany, but my motto is *you should be able to forgive, but you should not forget*.

SELECTED BIBLIOGRAPHY

Papers and Archives

The Imperial War Museum, London; The Association of Jewish Ex-service Men and Women (AJEX); the Association of Jewish Refugees; the Jewish Military Museum, London; the Public Record Office, Kew; the Royal Logistics Corps Museum; the National Army Museum; the Tank Museum; the Ilfracombe Museum and the North Devon Record Office.

In Germany: the archives of Verein für Geschichte und Kultur der Juden der Rheinlande (museum) in Königswinter near Bonn, and archives of Dachau Concentration Camp Memorial Site.

The official war diaries of the 8th King's Royal Irish Hussars, Public Record Office, ref: WO 171/843. Other files consulted at the Public Record Office: HO 396/37259 and PRO 396/37/260. Official regimental history: *A Short History of 7th Armoured Division, June 1943–July 1945*. *The Crossbelts* – the Journal of the 8th King's Royal Irish Hussars, 1945–6 and 1947–8.

Books and Memoirs

Ambrose, Tom. *Hitler's Loss: What Britain and America Gained from Europe's Cultural Exiles*, Peter Owen, 2001

Bartrop, Paul. *The* Dunera *Affair: A Documentary Resource Book*, Jewish Museum of Australia, 1990

Bellamy, Bill. *Troop Leader: A Tank Commander's Story*, Sutton Publishing, 2005

Bender, Edgar. *Reminiscences of the Pioneer Corps: 1940–1942*, unpublished.

Bentwich, Norman. *I Understand the Risks: The Story of the Refugees from Nazi Oppression who Fought in the British Forces in the World War*, Victor Gollancz, 1950

Berghahn, Marion. *Continental Britons: German-Jewish Refugees from Nazi Germany*, Berg Publishers, 1988

Blakeney, Michael. *Australia and the Jewish Refugees*, Croom Helm, 2000

Cresswell, Yvonne. *Living With the Wire: Civilian Internment in the Isle of Man during the Two World Wars*, Manx National Heritage, 1994

Distel, Barbara & Jakusch, Ruth (eds). *Concentration Camp Dachau*, Comité International de Dachau, Munich, 1978

Fitzroy, Olivia. *Men of Valour: The 3rd Volume of the History of the VIII King's Royal Irish Hussars 1927–1958*, C. Tinling & Co., 1961

Fry, Helen. *Freuds' War*, The History Press, 2009

———. 'The Germans who Fought for Britain' in *Military Illustrated*, December 2008

———. *Churchill's German Army*, The History Press, 2009

———. *Jews in North Devon during the Second World War*, Halsgrove, 2005

Gill, Alan. *Interrupted Journeys: Young Refugees from Hitler's Reich*, Simon & Schuster, 2004

Gillman, Peter & Gillman, Leni. *Collar the Lot: How Britain Interned and Expelled its Wartime Refugees*, Quartet Books, 1980

Gottlieb, Amy Zahl. *Men of Vision: Anglo-Jewry's Aid to Victims of the Nazi Regime 1933–1945*, Weidenfeld & Nicolson, 1998

Grenville, Anthony. *Continental Britons: Jewish Refugees from Nazi Europe*, The Jewish Museum, London, 2002

Hammond, Joyce. *Walls of Wire*, Rushworth, Tatura, 1990

Lafitte, Francois. *The Internment of Aliens*, Libris, 1988

Leighton-Langer, Peter. *X Steht für unbekannt: Deutsche und Österreicher in den Britischen Streitkräften im Zweiten Weltkrieg* (X Means Unknown: Germans and Austrians in the British Fighting Forces in the Second World War), Verlag, Berlin, 1999

Leighton-Langer, Peter. *The King's Own Loyal Enemy Aliens*, Vallentine Mitchell, 2006

Masters, Peter. *Striking Back*, Presidio, 1997

Neillands, Robin. *The Desert Rats: 7th Armoured Division 1940–1945*, Orion, 1995

Patkin, Benzion. *The* Dunera *Internees*, Cassell, 1979

Pearl, Cyril. *The* Dunera *Scandal*, Angus & Robertson, 1983

Perlès, Alfred. *Alien Corn*, George Allen & Unwin Ltd, 1944

Perry, Geoffrey. *When Life Becomes History*, White Mountain Press, 2002

Perry, Peter J. *An Extraordinary Commission: The Story of a Journey Through Europe's Disaster*, published by the author, 1997, distributed by T.J. Gillard Print Services, Bristol

Rauhut-Brungs, Leah & Wasser, Gabriele (eds). *Stadtrundgang durch Bonns jüdische Geschichte*, Verlag Roman Kovar, 2001

Rogers, Garry. *Interesting Times*, privately published autobiography, 1998

Rossney, Harry. *Grey Dawns: Illustrated Poems about Life in Nazi Germany, Emigration, and Active Service in the British Army during the War*, History Web Ltd, 2009

Sanders, Eric. *From Music to Morse*, History Web Ltd, 2009

Snowman, Daniel. *The Hitler Emigrés*, Pimlico, 2003

Stent, Ronald. *A Bespattered Page? The Internment of 'His Majesty's Most Loyal Enemy Aliens'*, Andre Deutsch, 1980

Travers, W (ed). *Arrival of HMT* Dunera *at Sydney*, Fiftieth Anniversary Year, The *Dunera* Association, September 1990

Ward, Kenneth. *And then the Music Stopped Playing*, Braiswick, 2006

Wasserstein, Bernard. *Britain and the Jews of Europe*, OUP, 1988

Winter, Barbara. *Stalag Australia*, Angus and Robertson, 1986

INDEX